Please return/renew this item by the last date shown.
Items may also be renewed by the internet*

https://library.eastriding.gov.uk

*Please note a PIN will be required to access this service
- this can be obtained from your library

THE
GREAT WAR
ILLUSTRATED
1914

THE
GREAT WAR
ILLUSTRATED
1914

*A Picture Editor's selection of 1,000 images
illustrating historic events in 1914*

WILLIAM LANGFORD

Pen & Sword
MILITARY

Dedicated to the One True Sovereign
who was disregarded by the nations when, in 1914, they elected to fight
among themselves on behalf of their own sovereignties

First published in Great Britain in 2013 by
PEN & SWORD MILITARY
an imprint of
Pen & Sword Books Ltd,
47 Church Street, Barnsley,
South Yorkshire.
S70 2AS

ISBN 9781781593462

A CIP catalogue record for this book is available
from the British Library

Designed by Factionpress
Printed and bound in India by Replika Press Pvt. Ltd.

Pen & Sword Books Ltd incorporates the imprints of
Pen & Sword Aviation, Pen & Sword Maritime,
Pen & Sword Military, Pen & Sword Select, Pen & Sword Military Classics,
Leo Cooper, Wharncliffe Local History

For a complete list of Pen & Sword titles please contact:
PEN & SWORD BOOKS LIMITED
47 Church Street, Barnsley, South Yorkshire, S70 2AS, England.
E-mail: enquiries@pen-and-sword.co.uk
Website: www.pen-and-sword.co.uk

Contents

Introduction   6

Chapter One   **Jealous Nations – Spoiling for a Fight** 9

Chapter Two   **Patriotism – The Bugle Calls, Salute the Flag!** 41

Chapter Three   **The Almighty's Decision – Which Side to Favour?** 75

Chapter Four   **Coming to Blows – August 1914** 91

Chapter Five   **Into the Fray – British at Mons** 155

Chapter Six   **Counter Punch – First Battle of the Marne** 191

Chapter Seven   **First Battle of the Aisne – First Battle of Ypres** 219

Chapter Eight   **Exchanging Broadsides – Fighting at Sea** 273

Chapter Nine   **Trench Warfare – Christmas and Not Over Yet** 335

Index   363

Introduction

Scholars and historians of succeeding generations following the one which lived through and experienced the horrors of the First World War have puzzled as to how it all came about. Professor A.J.P. Taylor stated, 'It is difficult, in fact, to discover any cause of hostility between the European Great Powers in the early summer of 1914.' There had been tension between them but the situation had calmed. Justification for nations becoming embroiled in the war, optimistically labelled by some as it got under way as 'the war to end all wars', seems fuzzy and confusing.

As the twentieth century began, Europe began to separate into two distinct camps forged by alliances between, on the one hand, the three centrally located European empires of Germany, Austria-Hungary and Italy, and, on the other, those of the nations ringed geographically around them. The Prussian statesman Otto von Bismarck had he been alive (he died just eighteen months prior to the twentieth century) would have viewed the situation with foreboding. Being the undoubted founder of the German nation he had been well aware of the danger of having potential enemies on two frontiers of his newly formed country and, through clever diplomacy, had averted that threat. True to Bismarck's concerns, and according to many historians, including Professor Taylor, the cause of the war was the system of alliances: on the one hand the German, Austria-Hungary and Italian – the so called Triple Alliance – faced off against a rival power bloc consisting of the French, British, and Russian nations – the Triple Entente. However, that arrangement could still have made for a peaceful world had the kings and national governments respected each other's sovereignties, after all they professed to be stalwarts of the Christian faith. Furthermore, those rulers were often interrelated, one with another, through marriage alliances.

Monarchs such as Kaiser Wilhelm II of Germany, Czar Nicholas II of Russia and Emperor Franz Joseph of Austria-Hungary were adherents to and bound by the signatures of their forebears to what was termed the Holy Alliance, which proclaimed that God had delegated them to oversee parts of Christendom. 'We Christian Kings,' wrote the Kaiser to the Czar of Russia, 'have one duty imposed upon us by Heaven, that is to uphold the principle of the divine right of kings.' Firmly endowed with such an arrogant conviction the supreme rulers in Europe could have been expected to exercise their autocratic authority with benevolence to avert outright conflict between their subjects.

Coupled with belief in the divinely ordered heads of state was the fact that at the start of the twentieth century the churches were well subscribed and attended. The clergy were acknowledged to be representatives of the suppliant laity interceding on their behalf before the presence of the Almighty. Those religious institutions, the various denominations, exercised undeniable influence over the masses and especially world rulers and governmental leaders. The thrust of their message purported to be one of universal love, forgiveness, tolerance and peace. With such powerful factors for peace in place, how could world war even be contemplated in the twentieth century?

Bearing this out, Winston Churchill wrote, 'The spring and summer of 1914 were marked in Europe by an exceptional tranquility.' The rivalry between Britain and Germany, which had existed in the years leading up to 1914, seemed to have settled down. As the year began 1914 was full of promise and Churchill further wrote with confidence, 'Germany seemed with us, set on peace.' Obviously, then, other factors were involved which caused men to suddenly, in a matter of days, abandon the Christian ethic of worldwide brotherhood in favour of hatred, and to subscribe to wholesale slaughter. Patriotism was clearly a factor.

Extreme patriotism, in the summer of 1914, acted like petrol vapour to a smouldering rag. Devotion to their particular nation manifested by citizens of European states, coupled with xenophobia, succeeded in working-up the peoples to enter into what would become four years of butchery. There was a spirit which operated with such intensity that in sweeping over the nations it prompted men to abandon their jobs and to descend en masse on the recruiting offices. They appeared eager – if indeed they had thought it through – to be taught how they might shed the blood of foreigners with bullet, bayonet and bomb, preferably on the away ground.

At the height of unashamed patriotism at the outbreak of war the gallant British Tommy was cast in the role of hero, rescuing defenceless Belgian women and children from the rapacious 'Hun'. There is no doubt that there were atrocities carried out against the civilian population by some among the one million plus German soldiers sweeping through Belgium. In such a situation, and against such acts of foulness, God, it was reasoned, was surely to be on the side of the Allies and would cause Tommy Atkins and his glorious allies to triumph over evil in the end.

Assisting the national cause, and to bolster patriotism, clergymen of the day, for their sermons, drew on Old Testament accounts of how the great Jehovah granted outstanding victories to His people Israel, even intervening with hailstones, flashflood and fire from Heaven on special occasions. Therefore, surely the virtuous Allies could expect no less.

The one reviled as the detestable invader rampaging through Belgium in the summer of 1914, the German soldier, for his part was sufficiently confident of the Almighty's favour. He was equipped with a slogan carried on his belt buckle that announced millions of times throughout Kaiser Wilhelm's army: *Gott Mit Uns* (God is with us).

In 1914 the long established monarchies and governments, the religious institutions, supported by big business and applauded by the press, capitalized on the unswerving patriotism and enthusiasm of the masses. In Britain national pride was exploited in order to swell the ranks of an army which was to proceed abroad and engage in four years of vicious battles in support of the sovereignty of the British Empire. Amazingly, just fourteen years earlier the fighting forces of eight nations were united in a common cause.

In June 1900, Boxer forces and Imperial Chinese troops had besieged diplomats, citizens and soldiers within the legations of Austria-Hungary, Belgium, Britain, France, Italy, Germany, Japan, Netherlands, Russia, Spain and the United States within the city of Peking. On 4 August a large relief force called the **Eight-Nation Alliance** marched upon Peking. The alliance force consisted of around 18,000 soldiers: Russian infantry, Cossacks and artillery; Japanese infantry; 3,000 British, mostly Indian infantry, cavalry and artillery; US soldiers and Marines with artillery; and a French brigade with artillery. Troops from Austria, Italy, and Germany were a part of this small relief army.

Thus, prior to taking up arms against each other the kings and emperors were bonded with western presidents in a common cause – exploitation of the Chinese people.

1103   A postcard depicting the three rulers of the Central Powers, Austro-Hungary, Germany and Turkey.

The Taylor Picture Library

In 2002 publisher Charles Hewitt acquired the photographic archive of military collector and medals dealer Peter N. Taylor of Barnsley and in so doing instantly obtained thousands of images of both the First and Second World Wars. With this book, *The Great War Illustrated 1914,* a selection of over 1,000 images is displayed on its pages; an identification number has been given the individual illustrations so that they may be ordered by authors, book designers, picture researchers and television and film programme makers. The images are all corrected and brought to the required specification and generous size requested by printers of books and magazines.

Peter Taylor has been dealing in medals and militaria for over twenty-five years throughout which he has had the foresight to buy up collections and albums of photographs, many of which were first generation press-release prints with the officially sanctioned caption on the back. In the eighties and nineties photographs of the Great War could be picked up for a few pence; now at arms fairs they may fetch up to £50 a print.

An example of a one hundred-year-old press release photograph with caption information provided on a label attached to the back (collectors may find that in many cases these have become detached over the years and lost). On this sample there are two rubber stamps indicating the issuer and user of the image. The Central Press Office of Farringdon Avenue, London, is requesting an acknowledgement should a newspaper or magazine reproduce the picture. The user, R. B. Brett & Son, was a publishing company based in Auckland, New Zealand with an office in Fleet Street, London.

The attached picture label on the back reads:
HOME COMING OF THE VICTIMS OF N. 13
The bodies of the fourteen victims of the submarine N. 13 who were killed in cowardly fashion by German destroyers, were brought ashore at Hull on Saturday from the Danish ship "Vidar". They were taken through the street to Paragon Station from whence they were sent to the homes of the relatives.
The picture shows the coffins covered with a mass of wreaths at the station with a guard of honour of sailors on one side and soldiers on the other.

Royal rulers of Europe gathered on the occasion of the funeral of Britain's Edward VII in 1910. Four years later when tensions between the Great Powers reached crisis point, some of them, instead of seeking peace between their governments, sought further power and signed declarations of war, plunging their subjects into four years of misery. Seated, left to right: Alfonso XIII of Spain, George V, Frederick VII of Denmark. Standing, left to right: Haakon VII of Norway, Ferdinand of Bulgaria, Manoel of Portugal, William II of Germany, George I of Greece, Albert of Belgium.

Chapter One: **Jealous Nations – Spoiling for a Fight**

966 Royal Navy Grand Fleet of battleships at full steam in the North Sea.

959 Western missionaries arrived in China with the soldiers and merchants from seven nations.

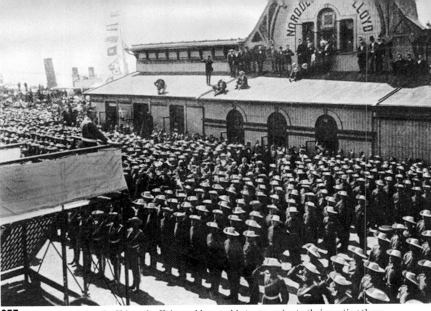
957 Germany's interest in China: the Kaiser addresses his troops prior to their posting there.

964 Boxer prisoners awaiting their fate.

958 Boxer prisoner locked in a cangue at a prison in Peking.

962 Six prisoners suffer a gradual death suspended in cangue frames.

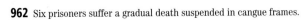

953 A remarkable sight, soldiers representing the eight nations involved in the exploitation of the Chinese people seen together: Left to right: infantryman Britain; American; Russian marine; British Indian cavalryman; German infantryman; French infantryman; Austrian sailor; Italian and Japanese infantrymen.

955 Americans, British and French are seen here after the relief of Peking in August 1900.
As the 20th Century began there occurred a remarkable instance of international cooperation when eight nations united in exploiting China. Little wonder that an uprising against them occurred. Many wanted these foreigners out of their country – some resorted to force and these freedom fighters became known as Boxers. Fighting broke out in 1900 and the various nationals found themselves under siege in their various consulates in Peking.

956 A Japanese firing squad engaged in shooting two prisoners to death. This is not volley firing but each soldier shoots indendently. The suffering of the two bound men can be imagined.

956 The Japanese preferred to decapitate their prisoners. A Japanese officer cleans his sword after executing four Chinese rebels.

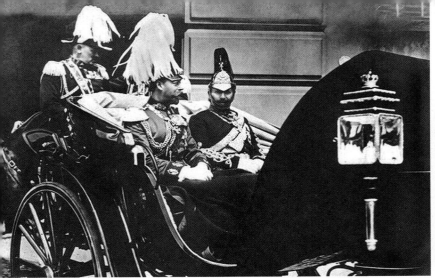

965 King George V and Kaiser Wilhelm II on the occasion of the German monarch's visit to Britain to observe British Army manoeuvres. The two kings have exchanged uniforms.

967 The Kaiser Wilhelm II and Winston Churchill, 1909 observing German Army manoeuvres near Würzburg.

975 The Kaiser at military manoeuvres, Germany, in 1906.

974 The Kaiser with Czar Nicholas on a hunting occasion in Germany.

976 The Czar Nicholas of Russia reviewing the Tscherkasky Regiment before 1914.

968 King George V talking to French General Foch during British Army manoeuvres at Cambridge in 1912.

970 In England the Kaiser and King George V consult the military manoeuvres schedule, having exchanged uniforms.

971 The Kaiser and King George V both in German uniforms for a review of troops in Germany.

971 Czar Nicholas and King George V.

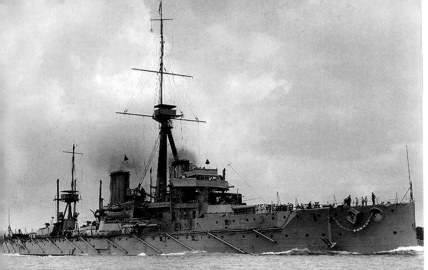

The Royal Navy's battleship HMS *Dreadnought* was first of a kind and triggered a naval arms race. Launched in 1906 *Dreadnaught* had such an impact that similar battleships built after her were referred to as 'dreadnoughts', and earlier battleships became known as 'pre-dreadnoughts'. Her design had two revolutionary features: an all-big-gun armament layout, with an unprecedented number of heavy-calibre guns, and steam turbine propulsion. Dreadnoughts became a symbol of national power, and renewed the naval arms race between the United Kingdom and Germany. Other nations, of course, had to have their own 'dreadnaughts'.

973 The 'ground-breaking' British battleship HMS *Dreadnaught* when launched made every other battleship obsolete.

978 Pre-dreadnaught battleship, HMS *Majestic*, flagship of the Channel Fleet from 1895-1903. She then served with the Atlantic Fleet (1906). At the outbreak of the Great War, *Majestic* became part of the 7th Battle Squadron of the Channel Fleet.

980 Winston Churchill, in an admiral's uniform, and Lord Morley in 1908.

983 Unashamed militarism practised by the Church of England. The Duke of Connaught reviewing the armed Church Lads Brigade in Hyde Park in 1908.

954 Winston Churchill made sure that Great Britain stayed ahead in the arms race.

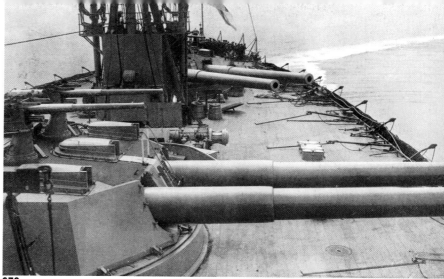

979 Stern guns of HMS *Dreadnaught*. Two turrets housing four of the 12-inch guns comprising the main armament of the new class of super battleship.

981 German Count Zeppelin's new airship undergoing trials over the town of Zurich. It flew from Lake Constance to Lucerne and back, 250 miles, in twelve hours. Here was a new instrument with which to wage war by dropping explosives on towns, troops and ships beneath, giving birth to the aerial bomb.

985 German High Seas Fleet manoeuvring at speed during a pre-war exercise.

984 The Kaiser in conference with Admiral von Tirpitz, German Naval Minister, and Admiral von Holtzendorf, Commander-in-Chief of the German High Seas Fleet.

986 SMS *Nassau* the first German 'dreadnaught', launched in 1906.

988 German naval officers having drinks in their quarters aboard a battleship.

987 A German naval rating beating The Tattoo.

989 German sentry 'presents arms' for the camera.

990 Army scheme in 1908, General Smith-Dorrien confers with his staff officers.

991 In the A manouevres in 1908 the 'invaders,' Blue side, are seen here positioned on a railway line.

992 Grenadier Guardsmen resting by the roadside during the war scheme in 1908.

994 Watering horses in the 1908 exercise.

992 Royal Engineers with the defending Red Army tap out a message via a mobile telegraph apparatus in 1908.

996 Adding realism to the exercises in 1908 howitzers for the defending Red Army, fire a barrage.

993 Infantry taking part in the war games march through the town of Alresford.

997 Observation contraption using a man-lifting kite designed by Samuel Franklin Cody. It would not be employed in the Great War.

998 Observation balloon section at work during German Army manoeuvres in 1908.

999 New equipment being tested by the French Army in 1908.

1006 German artillery observers during army exercises in 1914.

1005 The famous Zieten Hussars of the German Army.

1001 Another Dreadnaught Class ship launched September 1908, HMS *St Vincent*.

1000 French Army on manoeuvres at Blois on the Loire in 1908. Military and political leaders from other countries were invited to observe.

1004 German artillery observers during army exercises in 1914 testing new opitcal rangefinders.

1002 Dreadnaught *Minas Geraes* built for the Brazilian Navy at the Armstrong Yard, Elswick, Newcastle-on-Tyne

1007 The Kaiser at war games in the early summer of 1914. Note, along with the fanfare, the Taube scout plane, Zepplin and latest model artillery rangefinder.

1013 The Krupp foundary at Essen producing big guns for the German 'dreadnaught' type of battleship.

1016 Part of the rifle assembling section of the Birmingham Small Arms Company (B.S.A.).

1017 First shooting test of a Short Lee-Enfield Mk. III service rifle at the B.S.A. factory.

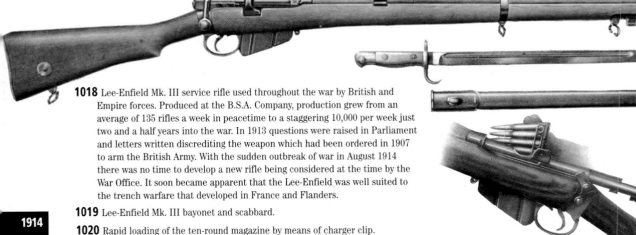

1018 Lee-Enfield Mk. III service rifle used throughout the war by British and Empire forces. Produced at the B.S.A. Company, production grew from an average of 135 rifles a week in peacetime to a staggering 10,000 per week just two and a half years into the war. In 1913 questions were raised in Parliament and letters written discrediting the weapon which had been ordered in 1907 to arm the British Army. With the sudden outbreak of war in August 1914 there was no time to develop a new rifle being considered at the time by the War Office. It soon became apparent that the Lee-Enfield was well suited to the trench warfare that developed in France and Flanders.

1019 Lee-Enfield Mk. III bayonet and scabbard.

1020 Rapid loading of the ten-round magazine by means of charger clip.

1015 The first aeroplane completed at the Daimler Works, the B.E.2c, shortly before war broke out in August 1914. War was to go into the skies for the first time.

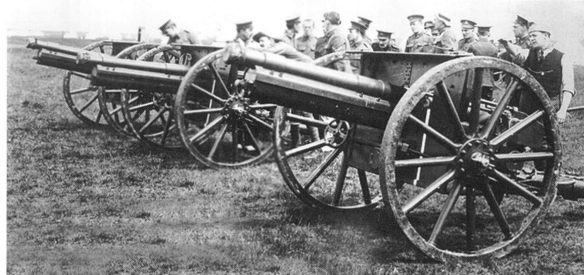

1017 Honorable Artillery Company at Fargo Camp, Aldershot, pre-war 1914. New recruits are being introduced to the British field gun.

1021 French submarine takes on torpedoes. Warfare was ready to go under the waves in the coming conflict.

1012 HMS *Daring* the first vessel to attain a speed of **29 knots**. Torpedo boat built for the Royal Navy by Thornycroft of Southampton.

1022 HMS *Desperate* the first vessel to attain a speed of **30 knots**. Built for the Royal Navy by Thornycroft of Southampton.

1025 HMS *Tarter* the first vessel to attain a speed of **37 knots**. Built for the Royal Navy by Thornycroft of Southampton.

1023 HMS *Albatross* the first vessel to attain a speed of **32 knots**.

The struggle for speed among the powers of the world is seen here in the boats. Britain kept ahead by a narrow margin.

1024 The *Usufumo*, Japanese destroyer which took the lead on water for a short period with a speed of **32 knots**.

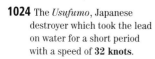

1026 July 1914, with war clouds gathering heads of nations begin strengthening alliances: The Czar of Imperial Russia (centre) visits the Imperial Romanian royals at Constanza. Left, Crown Prinz Carol and right, King Ferdinand. Romania waited two years before coming into the war on the side of the Allies.

1032 Alexis Romanov, born August 1904, shot July 1918.

1033 Emperor Francis Joseph of Austria. Born 1830 died November 1916. Elisabeth, his wife and consort, was murdered by an Italian anarchist in Geneva, Switzerland in 1898.

1038 Czar Nikolay Alexandrovich Romanov, born May 1868, deposed March 1917, shot July 1918.

1914

26

1027 Russian and Romanian imperial families at Constanza, July 1914. From left to right: Grand Duchess Maria of Russia; King Ferdinand of Romania; Grand Duchess Anastasia of Russia; unidentified; unidentified; unidentified; Prince Carol of Romania; Queen Elizabeth of Romania; Czar Nicholas of Russia; Grand Duchess Olga of Russia; (seated with baby, Prince Mircia of Romania). Seated centre: Czarina; Grand Duchess Tatiana of Russia; Princess Ileana of Romania. In front: Czarevitch Aleksey and Prince Nicholas of Romania.

It was gossip in the socialite press that Olga and Ferdinand were about to become engaged. However, Olga did not like the Romanian Crown Prince, despite encouragement from her mother the Czarina. And Olga claimed that Ferdinand fancied her younger sister Marie anyway. Czar Nicholas maintained that twenty-year-old Olga was too young. Did he know about Ferdinand's attraction to his fifteen-year-old daughter Marie?

1031 Anastasia Romanov, born June 1901, shot July 1918.

1030 Marie Romanov, born June 1899, shot July 1918.

1029 Tatiana Romanov, born May 1897, shot July 1918.

1028 Olga Romanov, born November 1895, shot July 1918.

1034 Archduke Francis Ferdinand his wife Sophia and their three children Prince Ernest, Prince Maximilian and Princess Sophia.

1037 Royal beauty Elisabeth Amalie Eugenie (Sisi), Austrian consort born December 1837, was assassinated by an Italian anarchist when he stabbed her whilst she was walking in the street in Geneva, September 1898.

1039 King of Portugal Dom Carlos I. Shot twice and killed while riding in an open-top carriage through the streets of Lisbon, February 1908.

1040 Crown Prince Luiz Philippe hit twice in the face and chest by another assassin armed with a rifle on the same occasion, Lisbon, February 1908.

Previous Assassinations of Heads of State and family members
1801 – Paul, Czar of Russia
1865 – Abraham Lincoln
1876 – Abdul Aziz, Sultan of Turkey
1881 – Alexander II, Czar of Russia
1881 – General Garfield US President
1894 – President Carnot of France
1898 – Elizabeth, Empress of Austria
1900 – Humbert I, King of Italy
1901 – President McKinley
1903 – Alexander I, King of Servia
1903 – Queen Draga, of Servia

1043 King George V and Queen Mary visiting Nottingham, June 1914.

1046 Procession of Royal motor cars leaving Hamilton Palace on King George V and Queen Mary's visit to Scotland, July 1914.

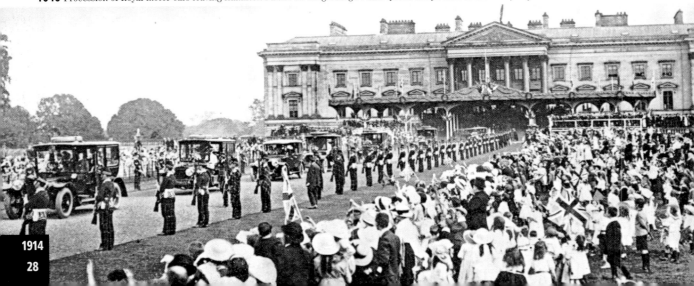

1041 Emmeline Pankurst handing out leaflets in her campaign to get women the vote.

1042 Emmeline Pankurst under arrest.

1043 King George V and Queen Mary visit Glasgow, July 1914 and the king lays a foundation stone for new building.

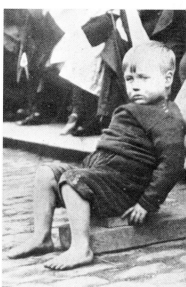

1047 Waiting to see the king can be very boring.

1044 King George V inspects a guard of honour at Perth, July 1914.

1049 Photograph taken from the royal yacht, *Alexandra*. The two destroyers in the foreground are the *Lizard* and the *Jackal*. In the background can be seen the 3rd and 4th Battle Squadrons. The King's last peace-time inspection of the Fleet, July 1914.

1051 The Naval Inspection of the Fleet in July 1914 was described as an Official Test Muster – the thunder clouds of war were gathering and the final days of world peace were counting down.

1052 Eight Naval seaplanes taking part in the Spithead Review of 1914. This was the first occasion that floatplanes took part in the ceremony.

King George led his fighting ships out towards the open sea, and taking up a position the whole fleet defiled before him. The royal yacht then proceeded towards the open waters of the Channel and witnessed manouevres by the destroyers. An airship hovered overhead and for the first time naval aircraft flew over the fleet. At a prearranged moment big guns of the fleet boomed out in salute.

1050 Latest 'Dreadnaughts' HMS *Iron Duke* and HMS *Marlborough*. The King's last peace-time inspection of the Fleet, July 1914.

1048 The royal yacht, *Alexandra*, with King George V on board sails past HMS *New Zealand* during the King's Inspection of the Fleet, July 1914.

1053 Pusher type seaplane photographed during the King's Inspection of the Fleet, July 1914.

1054 The Okhrana cafe in Belgrade, in which the murderers of Austrian heir to the throne forged their plans.

1055 Three conspirators bent on murder. Gavrilo Princip who would fire the shots is on the right.

1056 Map of pre-war europe.

PREWAR EUROPE

1057 Target for the assassins, Franz Ferdinand; his wife Sophie would also get in the line of fire. With their children, Ernest (left), Sophi and Maximilian.

1063 Looking down on the town of Sarajevo, capitol of the territory annexed by Austria in 1908.

1058 Archduke Franz Ferdinand and Princess von Hohenberg are welcomed to Sarajevo by the mayor, Fehim Âurãiç.

Governor of the Austrian provinces of Bosnia and Herzegovina had invited Franz Ferdinand to the opening of a hospital. The visit would be risky, Emperor Franz Josef, had been the subject of an assassination attempt in 1911.

1059 After freshening-up and changing the Archduke and his wife leave the town hall for a tour of Sarajevo in an open-topped car.

1060 The Archduke has changed to a feathered hat as he and his wife leave the town hall for a tour of Sarajevo in an open-topped car.

1070 Franz Ferdinand and Sophie take their seats in the open-topped car.

The royal couple had arrived in Sarajevo by train at around 10 am, Sunday 28 June 1914. After a brief stop at the town hall they travelled in a motorcade of five cars. Six conspirators lined the route along the Appel Quay, each one with instructions to try to kill Franz Ferdinand when the royal car reached his position. The first conspirator lost his nerve. Then a student member of the gang threw a hand grenade at the Archduke's car which exploded under the wheel of the fourth car wounding two of the occupants. Franz Ferdinand decided to go to the hospital and visit the injured. On the way there the driver took a right turn into Franz Josef Street. Princip was standing near Moritz Schiller's cafe when Franz Ferdinand's car stopped, having taken the wrong turn. Upon realizing his mistake, the driver braked, and began to reverse giving Princip his opportunity. At a distance of about five feet Princip shot Franz Ferdinand in the neck and Sophie in the abdomen. They were both dead before 11 am.

1064 The target car drove along Appel Quay and when it reached the spot marked, corner of Franz Josef Street, Princip fired at the couple killing both.

1069 One of the many artistic impressions of the killing produced at the time.

1072 Princip is marched away his suicide capsule having failed to work – it was out of date and the cyanide had deteriorated.

1065 Spirits seem to be high as the motorcade leaves the town hall.

1066 The target car as it approached the Latin Bridge over the Miljacka river.

1069 A German version of the event. (Note the feathered hat which was correct.)

1067 Princip under arrest following the killings.

1075 Nedeljko Cabrinoviç handcuffed and held by three tall secret police.

Princip and Cabrinoviç were captured and interrogated by the police. They eventually gave the names of their fellow conspirators.

1073 Princip showing signs of his interrogation.

1074 Nedeljko Cabrinoviç threw the bomb that seriously injured two people in the car and wounded bystanders. His cyanide capsule was out of date and he was captured after jumping in the river which was only a few inches deep.

1078 A queue waiting to view the Lying in State at the Burgkapelle, Vienna.

Every member of the Black Hand Gang, Young Bosnia, involved in the murder was identified; eight were arrested and charged with treason and the murder of Archduke Franz Ferdinand; one escaped capture, Muhamed Mehmedbasiç, and fled to Serbia. All were found guilty. Under Austro-Hungarian law, capital punishment could not be imposed on someone who was under the age of twenty when they had committed the crime, consequently, Princip, Cabrinoviç and Grabez received the maximum penalty of twenty years. Vaso Cubriloviç was sentenced to 16 years and Cvjetko Popoviç to 13 years. Veljko Cubriloviç, Misko Jovanoviç and Danilo Iliç were executed 3 February 1915. Trifko Grabez died of tuberculosis in February, 1918. Gavrilo Princip died of tuberculosis a few months before the First World War ended. Last of the conspirators, Vaso Cubriloviç, died in 1990.

1076 The team of assassins in court. All were found guilty and three were sentenced to death.

1089 Austrian 19-cm artillery piece with its complement of thirty gunners. This and other guns threatened the Serbian city of Belgrade across the Danube.

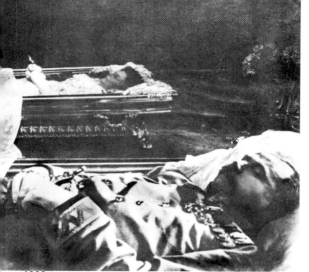
1080 Lying in State at the Burgkapelle, Vienna.

1079 Lying in State at the Burgkapelle, Vienna. The Archduke and his consort among a forest of candles in the Royal Chapel.

Princip, Nedjelko Cabrinoviç and Grabez were suffering from tuberculosis and knew they would not live long. Consequently they were willing to give their life for what they believed was a good cause, Bosnia-Herzegovina achieving independence from Austro-Hungary.

Veljko Cubriloviç, Misko Jovanoviç and Danilo Iliç were executed 3 February 1915.

1081 Belgian Fabrique Nationale Model 1910.

The pistol that introduced death and maiming to millions of people was a little FN pocket automatic holding eight rounds.

1085 Veljko Cubriloviç. **1086** Misko Jovanoviç. **1084** Danilo Iliç.

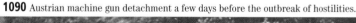
1090 Austrian machine gun detachment a few days before the outbreak of hostilities.

1087 Types making up the army of the Austro-Hungarian Empire in 1914: (left to right)

Uhlan Landwehr (militia)
Austrian Landwehr (militia)
Bosnian Rifleman
Austrian Rifleman
Hungarian Infantryman
Hungarian Infantryman
Tyrolese Sharpshooter
Bosnian Infantry
Hungarian Infantryman
Hungarian Hussar
Hussar Landwehr (militia)
Hungarian Rifleman
Mounted Rifleman
Bosnian Dragoon
Marine

The Austro-Hungarian Empire ruled over numerous language groups and religiously diverse peoples and not all were eager to fight for the Empire's enemies. This mix would prove to be a weakness in the coming conflict.

Franz-Josef, Emperor of Austria-Hungary, wrote to the Kaiser of Germany:

According to all the evidence so far brought to light, the Sarajevo affair was not merely the bloody deed of a single individual, but was the result of a well-organized conspiracy, the threads of which can be traced to Belgrade and although it will probably prove impossible to get evidence of the complicity of the Serbian Government, there can be no doubt that its policy, directed towards the unification of all countries under the Serbian flag, is responsible for such crimes, and that a continuation of such a state of affairs constitutes an enduring peril for my house and my possessions.

1092 Kaiser Wilhelm II of Germany.

1091 Emperor Franz Josef of Austro-Hungary.

1093 Austro-Hungary navy operating in the Adriatic Sea. Italy was its rival in that area and dreadnaught building had taken its toll on the finances of both nations.

The ten nigh impossible to meet demands made upon Serbia by Austria

1. To suppress all publications inciting hatred of Austria-Hungary and which were directed against her territorial integrity.
2. To dissolve forthwith the Narodna Odbrana ['National Defence' – formed in 1908 to present Serbia's cause to the world]; and to confiscate all its means of propaganda; to treat similarly all societies engaged in propaganda against Austria-Hungary, and to prevent their revival in another form.
3. To eliminate from the Serbian educational system anything which might foment such propaganda.
4. To dismiss all officers or officials guilty of such propaganda, whose names might subsequently be communicated by Vienna.
5. To accept the 'collaboration in Serbia' of Austria-Hungarian officials in suppressing this subversive movement against the monarchy's territorial integrity.
6. To open a judicial inquiry into the murders, and allow delegates of Austria-Hungary to take part in this.
7. To arrest without delay Major Tankosic and Milan Ciganovic, implicated by the Sarajevo inquiry.
8. To put an effectual stop to Serbian frontier officials sharing in the 'illicit traffic in arms and explosives', and to dismiss officials at Sabac and Loznica who had helped the murderers to cross over.
9. Give explanations regarding the unjustifiable language used by Serbian officials after the murder.
10. To notify Vienna without delay of the execution of all the above measures.

977 A cartoon style map of the land-locked country of Serbia (Servia) surrounded by territories ruled over by the House of Hapsburg. Serbia's capitol, Belgrade, was in the front line positioned on the River Danube.

1094 The Serbian government in session at the Skupstchina, Belgrade City Hall during a previous crisis in 1908 when the country was under threat by Austria.

1097 Count Berchtold, Austrian Minister of Foreign Affairs.

1095 King Peter I of Serbia.

1096 Nikola P. Pasiç Prime Minister of Serbia.

1098 Sergei Sazonoff Minister of Foreign Affairs, Serbia.

Telegram from German Chancellor Bethmann-Hollweg to the Emperor of Austro-Hungary: *As far as concerns Serbia, His Majesty of course cannot interfere in the dispute now going on between Austria-Hungary and that country, as it is a matter not within his competence. The Emperor Franz-Joseph may, however, rest assured that His Majesty will faithfully stand by Austria-Hungary as is required by the obligations of this alliance and of his ancient friendship.*

1. July 25-26 — Austria-Hungary breaks off diplomatic relations with Serbia and mobilizes its armed forces.
2. July 26 — British government attempts to organize a conference to settle Serbian problem.
3. July 28 — Austria-Hungary declares war on Serbia.
4. July 29 — Russia begins to mobilize in support of Serbia.
5. July 30 — Germany warns Russia to stop mobilizing and refuses to confirm adherence to Belgian neutrality.
6. July 31 — Russia orders general mobilization. Germany demands Russia to halt.
7. August 1 — Germany declares war on Russia.
8. August 1 — Belgium and France mobilize.
9. August 2 — Germany demands that Belgium allows transit of troops across her territory.
10. August 3 — Germany invades Belgium and declares war on France.
11. August 4 — Britain declares war on Germany.

1100 German Chancellor, Bethmann-Hollweg.

1099 Albert King of the Belgians.

1101 British Prime Minister Herbert Asquith.

1102 British Foreign Secretary Sir Edward Grey.

Chapter Two: Patriotism – The Bugle Calls, Salute the Flag!

1103 War fever infects these children on the streets of London.   **1104** German artillery passing through the Brandenburg Gate, Berlin, August 1914.

1109 Russian General Vladimir Sukhomlinov, Minister of War; he and the Czar's General Staff drew up plans for war.

1106 Russian artillery pictured during the mobilization of the Russian army.

1109 General Paul von Rennenkampf, commanded the Russian First Army.

1105 Russian cavalry during the mobilization of the army in support of Serbia, the 'brother' nation whose sovereignty was under threat from the Austro-Hungarian Empire.

1111 Russia was fielding the largest army ever seen with a total of 115 infantry divisions and 38 cavalry divisions with an artillery numbering 7,900 guns.

1108 Nicholas Nikolaevich Romanov, supreme commander of the Russian forces.

1110 General Alexander Samsonov, commanded the Russian Second Army.

1112 Target practice for Russian infantrymen during mobilization, July 1914.

1118 Crowds before the Berlin Palace on the evening of mobilization 1 August 1914.

1113 The fateful message arriving at Reuters, 'the world's news agency', reporting the declaration of war on Imperial Russia by the German Empire.

1114 Kaiser Wilhelm II with his generals in the field on the outbreak of hostilities.

1115 The German Crown Prince takes the salute on the outbreak of war.

1119 The Kaiser greets the crowd from the balcony of the Berlin Palace on the evening of German mobilization 1 August 1914.

1120 Men of the Territorial Army provide escort for ammunition being moved from the depot near the Serpentine in Hyde Park to London Bridge Station.

1121 Territorials marching out of their summer camp at Ashridge Park, Berkhamstead, July 1914. Battalions were recalled from summer camps as the crisis in Europe deteriorated.

1122 The two-week-long summer camps for Territorials were interrupted in July 1914 and the battalions were recalled to their depots. Here a Signals Company leads the Regimental Band out of Ashridge Park, Berkhamstead as news of the deteriorating situation in Europe became known.

Sir Edward Goschen has been informed by Sir Edward Grey that His Majesty The King of the Belgians has addressed to His Majesty King George an appeal for diplomatic intervention on behalf of Belgium.

His Majesty's Government are also informed that a Note has been delivered to the Belgian Government by the German Government proposing friendly neutrality entailing free passage through Belgian territory and promising to maintain at the conclusion of peace the independence and integrity of the Kingdom and its possessions, threatening to treat Belgium as an enemy in case of refusal. It was requested that an answer might be returned within twelve hours.

His Majesty's Government also understand that this request has been categorically refused by Belgium as a flagrant violation of the Law of Nations.

Sir Edward Grey states that His Majesty's Government are bound to protest against this violation of a Treaty to which Germany is a party in common with themselves and that they must request an assurance that the demand made upon Belgium will not be proceeded with and that Germany will respect the neutrality of Belgium.

Sir Edward Goschen is instructed to ask for an immediate reply.

BERLIN, August 4, 1914.

British Ambassador in Berlin, Sir Edward Goschen, received his instructions. In his last conversation with German Chancellor Theobald von Bethmann-Hollweg before asking for his passports, 4 August 1914, Bethmann famously expressed his astonishment that England would go to war for 'a scrap of paper' (the 1839 treaty guaranteeing Belgium's neutrality).

1124 The Hon Rupert Guiness at the inspection of the Royal Naval Reserve, August 1914.

1125 The Boy Scout movement was founded in 1908 by Baden Powell. The new para-military organization proved its worth when Scouts acted as messengers. Mounted Scouts are seen outside Victoria Station, London.

1132 Mobilization of the Royal Naval Reserve on the south-east coast. Preparations for war were pushed through with all urgency. The sailors depicted here appear happy to be called to their depot at Portsmouth and are being cheered off by their family and friends gathered on the quayside.

1129 A sailor bids farewell to his family at Waterloo Station as he leaves to join his ship.

1126 For the first time in history aeroplanes were about to play a significant role in warfare. Here a propeller in its box is being taken to Eastchurch where army military aviators had been assembled. These are Royal Engineers in the convoy to Eastchurch.

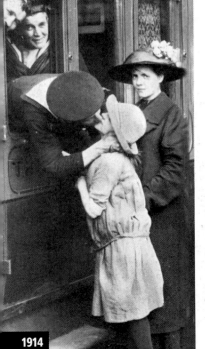

1128 A sergeant and his daughter at London Bridge.

1130 Men of the Royal Artillery taking their gun to the railway goods yard at Nine Elms.

1127 As the crisis came to a head Cowes week was cancelled and sailors from the regatta yachts left for Portsmouth.

1131 Territorial Army soldiers at London Bridge where they assisted in the mobilization taking place in the nation's capital.

1135/1136/1137/1138 On Friday 31 July members arriving at the Stock Exchange found a notice attached to the doors informing them: 'The House will be closed until further notice. The Press will be notified the day before the House is reopened'. Rumours were rife among the crowd of jobbers and brokers who had come to Throgmorton Street not knowing of the closure. One story was to the effect that thirty firms would be hammered were the Exchange to open for business while ever the present crisis lasted.

SUPPLEMENT
TO
The London Gazette
Of TUESDAY, the 4th of AUGUST, 1914.

Published by Authority.

WEDNESDAY, 5 AUGUST, 1914.

A STATE OF WAR

His Majesty's Government informed the German Government on August 4th, 1914, that, unless a satisfactory reply to the request of His Majesty's Government for an assurance that Germany would respect the neutrality of Belgium was received by midnight of that day, His Majesty's Government would feel bound to take all steps in their power to uphold that neutrality and the observance of a treaty to which Germany was as much a party as Great Britain

The result of this communication having been that His Majesty's Ambassador at Berlin had to ask for his passports, His Majesty's Government have accordingly formally notified the German Government that a state of war exists between the two countries as from 11 p.m. to-day.

Foreign Office,
August 4th, 1914.

1133 Crowds outside Buckingham Palace waiting for the British ultimatum to Germany to expire. They cheered King George, Queen Mary and the Prince of Wales as the hour passed midnight and a state of War existed with Germany as from 4 of August 1914. A popular war greeted with wild enthusiasm.

1134 Britain declared war on Tuesday 4 August 1914 and the following day the official declaration appeared in a supplement to *The London Gazette*, the official publication of the Government.

1139 Recruiting offices were soon swamped by men clamouring to join the Army and Navy. This is the scene at Whitehall offices, London, August 1914.

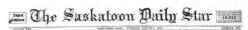

The Saskatoon Daily Star

Germany Declares War on Belgium
Germany Decided to Reject British Ultimatum

MARTIAL LAW PROCLAIMED IN GREAT BRITAIN

Germany Appeals to Italy To Stand In With Her

PREM. BORDEN CONFERS WITH GOV.-GENERAL

PREMIER ASQUITH CONFIRMS SENDING OF AN ULTIMATUM TO GERMANY

Requests the Same Guarantee of Belgian Neutrality as Given to France

1154 War news sweeps around the world as events unrolled.

1151 A German regiment marches through the streets of Berlin bound for the frontier.

1155 A crowd in Munich, 2 August, cheers the outbreak of war. Circled is Adolf Hitler.

1152 An enthusiastic crowd in Berlin cheer the declaration of war.

1153 This group in Berlin are reading the latest government bulletin concerning the war.

1160 A mother adjusts her son's equipment before he leaves.

Quotation from Lord Kitchener's Speech:

"It has been well said that in every man's life there is one supreme hour to which all earlier experience moves and from which all future results may be reckoned. For every individual Briton, as well as for our national existence, that solemn hour is now striking. Let us take heed to the great opportunity it offers, and which most assuredly we must grasp now and at once, or never. Let each man of us see that we spare nothing, shirk nothing, shrink from nothing, if only we may lend our full weight to the impetus which shall carry to victory the cause of honour and of our freedom."

"GOD SAVE THE KING."

1159 An extract from Lord Kitchener's speech to the nation.

1158 Lord Kitchener was appointed Secretary of State for War and he predicted the conflict would last at least three years and would require huge new armies to defeat Germany.

AUGUST 8TH, 1914.

Your King and Country Need You.

A CALL TO ARMS.

An addition of 100,000 men to his Majesty's Regular Army is immediately necessary in the present grave National Emergency.

Lord Kitchener is confident that this appeal will be at once responded to by all those who have the safety of our Empire at heart.

TERMS OF SERVICE.

General Service for a period of 3 years or until the war is concluded.
Age of Enlistment between 19 and 30.

HOW TO JOIN.

Full information can be obtained at any Post Office in the Kingdom or at any Military depot.

GOD SAVE THE KING!

1141 First newspaper advertisement, 8 August 1914.

1149 Lord Kitchener leaving the Guild Hall with the Lord Mayor inspects the guard.

1161 'It will be over by Christmas' was the popular cry. A jubilant crowd in Trafalgar Square, August 1914 (spot the woman).

1206 War precautions on the streets of London: sentries provided by the Civil Service Battalion at the Strand entrance to Somerset House.

1205 On the morning of 6 August 1914 the German Ambassador, Prince Karl Max Lichnowsky and his wife leave. He had done all he could to prevent war breaking out and blamed the policies of his own country for causing it 'if war breaks out it will be the greatest catastrophe the world has ever seen' he wrote in a telegram. Indicating the esteem in which he was held by the British a military guard of honour saluted his departure; a rare privilege in the circumstances.

1156 The most well-known poster image ever.

At the start of the Great World War, Lord Kitchener became Secretary of State for War, and a Cabinet Minister. One of the few to foresee a long conflict, he organized the largest volunteer army that Britain, and indeed the world, had seen and a significant expansion of material productions with which to fight Germany on the Western Front. His commanding image, on recruiting posters demanding 'Your country needs you!', remains with us, recognized and parodied to this day.

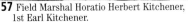

1157 Field Marshal Horatio Herbert Kitchener, 1st Earl Kitchener.

1150 Recruits taking the oath at the Central Recruiting Depot, Whitehall. The Bible was thus employed like a talisman in the patriotic spirit.

1171 Newly enlisted men walking from the recruiting offices to their training camps.

1142 Lapel badge issued to the battalions of 'Old Boys' of the University and Public School Brigade in lieu of uniforms.

1172 New recruits to the University and Public School Brigade wearing the lapel identification badge. They are seated on building materials which have recently arrived for building huts to accommodate them.

1144 London Transport buses arrive at Hyde Park to take new recruits of the University and Public School Brigade to Epsom, 18 September 1914.

1914

54

1169 Men being enlisted into a London regiment and taking the 'King's Shilling'.

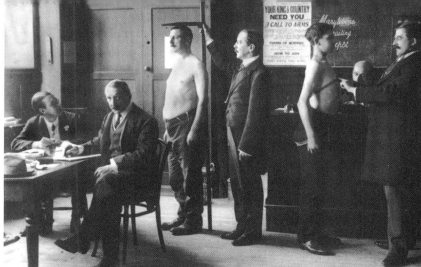

1170 Men being given a medical examination at Marleybone grammar school, London.

1140 The first poster for the raising of an entire infantry brigade from among university and public school 'Old Boys'. They would become 16th Battalion Middlesex Regiment; 18th, 19th, 20th and 21st Royal Fusiliers battalions.

UNIVERSITY & PUBLIC SCHOOLS BRIGADE

5000 MEN AT ONCE

The Old Public School and University Men's Committee makes an urgent appeal to their fellow Public School and University men to at once enlist in these battalions, thus upholding the glorious traditions of their Public Schools & Universities.

TERMS OF SERVICE.

Age on enlistment 19 to 35, ex-soldiers up to 45, and certain ex non-commissioned officers up to 50. Height 5 ft. 3 in. and upwards. Chest 34 in. at least. Must be medically fit.

General Service for the War.

Men enlisting for the duration of the War will be discharged with all convenient speed at the conclusion of the War.

PAY AT ARMY RATES.

and all married men or widowers with children will be accepted, and will draw separation allowance under Army Conditions.

HOW TO JOIN.

Men wishing to join should apply at once, personally, to the Public Schools & Universities Force, 66, Victoria Street, Westminster, London, S.W., or the nearest Recruiting Office of this Force.

GOD SAVE THE KING !

1143 Major-General Sir Francis Lloyd reviewing the University and Public Schools (U.P.S.) volunteers in Hyde Park.

1145 The U.P.S. (University and Public School Brigade) in Epsom High Street, 19 September 1914.

1145 Men of the U.P.S. (University and Public School Brigade) building their huts at Woodcote Camp.

1148 Men of the U.P.S. (University and Public School Brigade) learning to dig trenches.

1177 Press-ups for men of the U.P.S. (University and Public School Brigade). They were referred to as Kitchener's men in the popular press.

1146 Woodcote Camp under construction to house men of the U.P.S. (University and Public School Brigade).

1173 Brigadier-General R. Gordon Gilmour, CB, CVO, DSO commanding the U.P.S. Brigade.

1174 Woodcote Camp with the U.P.S. in residence.

1175 This platoon of the U.P.S. is under the command of Lieutenant Frank Foster, a famous cricketer who played for Warwickshire and England. He appears to be giving the command 'eyes front!' Note the mix of civvies and khaki.

1176 Major R. Hermon-Hodge, MVO, Brigade Major. U.P.S. (University and Public School Brigade)

1179 New recruits to the Lincolnshire Regiment under instruction for rifle handling. In their own clothes but the rifles are up-to-date Lee Enfield Mk IIIs.

1180 Non-commissioned officers of the New Army undergoing instruction in the art of physical training at the gymnasium, Aldershot.

1181 Recruits of the New Army are put through their paces before an admiring crowd in a public park.

1182 The first 'Pals' Battalion to be formed was the Stockbroker Battalion; when the Stock Exchange closed its doors and men were put out of employment General Rawlinson sought permission for them to join the army and be allowed to serve together. This – friends together – was quickly followed by Liverpool. It was Lord Derby of Liverpool who first used the term 'Pals' in a speech on 28 August 1914. Here the ex-Stockbrokers give three cheers for Field Marshal Lord Roberts VC at an inspection of Kitchener's men at Temple Gardens. Lord Roberts 'Bobs' died 14 November 1914 (aged 82).

1183 Because of the vast numbers enlisting in Kitchener's New Army, uniforms, rifles and equipment were not immediately available. Khaki material was quickly used up and Post-Office blue was used instead. Obsolete ammunition pouches, belts and straps were issued to the new recruits and Lee-Metford rifles – not to be fired, for drill purposes only – armed most of the new battalions. These rifles, remnants from the Boer War, were scarce. These are men of the 8th Battalion Leicestershire Regiment drilling at Woking wearing blue and equipped with old belts and pouches.

1184 The King's Liverpool Regiment at bayonet practice at Aldershot. Peaked hats in short supply.

1185 Practising pistol shooting the crypt of Kennington Parish Church.

1186 NCOs of the 11th Hussars instructing new recruits in rudimentaries of rifle drill.

1188 'Longest way up and shortest way down', a recruit to the 17th Battalion, Middlesex Regiment, is instructed on how to salute an officer.

1187 His Majesty King George V, accompanied by Lord Kitchener reviewing recruits at Aldershot.

1189 German Reservists, arrested at Folkestone before they could embark for German occupied Belgium, being marched away for internment.

1191 The fortunes of war: the former London offices of the German shipping company, Hamburg-Amerika Line, transformed into a recruiting office for the British Army.

1192 Shops bearing German and Austrian names attacked in Paris. These are the premises of an Austrian jeweller.

1190 German vessel, the *Marie Leonhardt*, captured before she could sail for Germany. Her cargo, now spoils of war, is being unloaded.

1193 A German agent arrested after being caught spying on one of the docks at Montreal, Canada. The Canadian authorities had carefully guarded against the threat of agents operating on their territory. Member countries of the British Empire mobilized men and resources in support of Great Britain.

1194 Ready for the great adventure now on offer in Europe. No. 1 Troop, 12th Manitoba Dragoons. The Dominion of Canada had made arrangements to raise an Expeditionary Force of over 20,000 men to be sent to the United Kingdom immediately.

1198 The Bengal Lancers of whom Earl Curzon said, to an audience in Glasgow, 'I would like to see the lancers of the Bengal Lancers fluttering down the streets of Berlin'.

1199 Gurkhas, smallest of the Indian contingent, yet they were destined to become a firm favourite of the British 'Tommy'.

1195 An Expeditionary Force of over 20,000 men to be sent from Australia to the United Kingdom immediately.

1196 Sir Pertab Singh, although 70 years old he went with Indian troops to fight for the King Emperor (he went with his 16 year old nephew the Maharajah of Jodhpur).

1200 John Redmond MP presents colours to the Maryborough Corps of Nationists, having declared that Irish volunteers, both Nationalist and Ulster, could be relied upon to defend Ireland in the present crisis.

1197 The Camel Corps commanded by the Maharajah of Bikaner.

1215 Dressed up and ready for the Big Adventure: the advance guard of Canada's 100,000 men, the Moose Jaw Legion of Frontiersmen which was absorbed into Princess Patricia's Light Infantry. Prior to the war this outfit had been raised and equipped by Montreal millionaire Hamilton Gaunt from among men who liked the glamour of a Stetson hat, boots and breeches, and the packing of a revolver holster.

1216 New Zealanders embarking at Christchurch for service in Egypt and to guard the Suez Canal.

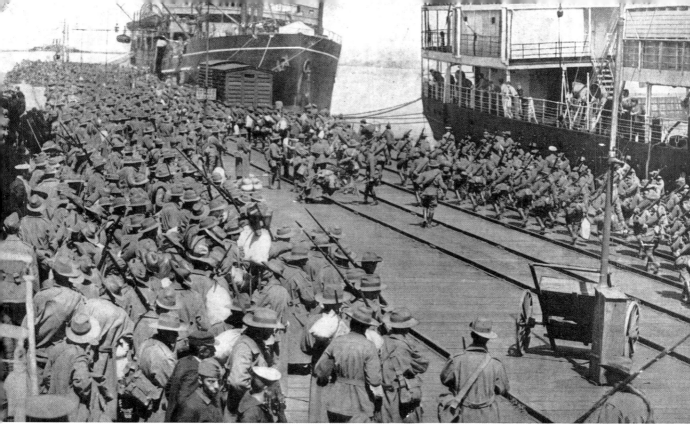

1217 Men of the Australian Imperial Force embarking at Melbourne for service in Europe on the Western Front. However, en route the destination was changed to Egypt.

1219 The New Zealand contingent embarking on transports at Christchurch.

1218 Major General Sir William Throsby Bridges commanded the AIF.

1221/1223/1222 South Africa and the men of the Transvaal Scottish take their leave of their loved ones to take part in the fighting.

1224 A party of London Hospital nurses at Charing Cross railway station about to leave for the south coast to care for the flow of wounded beginning to arriving from Belgium and France in growing numbers.

1225 A strip of three photographs showing Red Cross voluntary workers at Devonshire House, Picadilly, London. The original caption says 'engaged on their various duties'.

1226 Red Cross voluntary workers at Devonshire House, Picadilly, London, sorting out beds, blankets and pillows.

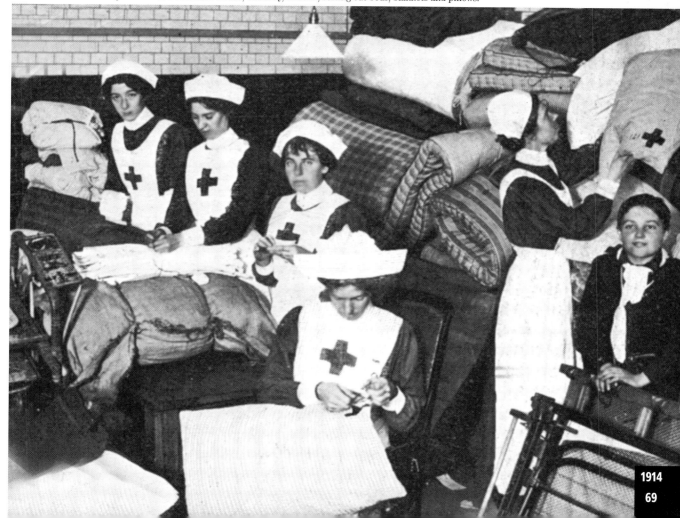

1201 A ladies' Red Cross sewing meeting in Claridges Hotel, London. They are making woollen shirts for use in Lord Tredegar's yacht which was to operate as a relief ship to the hospital ships on the French and Belgian coasts. Queen Mary had issued an appeal for all sewing guilds to cooperate with her in the supply of garments for the soldiers and sailors.

1202 'Back from the field of honour' runs the caption with this photograph: a party of British soldiers arriving at Salisbury Road School, Plymouth, in a converted omnibus, 31 August 1914. They were wounded men from the Middlesex and Royal Scots regiments, which were stationed at Plymouth when the war began a matter of a few weeks earlier. By this time there were 300 wounded at Woolwich, 316 in the London Hospital and 140 at Bishop Stortford. The following day, 1 September, 300 wounded arrived at Brighton and about 120 at both Portsmouth and Birmingham.

ARE YOU DOING YOUR SHARE TO WIN THE FIGHT AND KEEP GREAT BRITAIN FREE ?

Mr R. Pearson, a Portsmouth motor manufacturer, has given his services.

In this group (on the left) are two teachers, Messrs. Watkins and Mr Burns, a tailor. All trades and professions in Portsmouth and Southsea are providing men for service.

Mr P. Kiln, a Southsea motor dealer, is now a dispatch rider.

The women of Portsmouth are determined to give the men all the support they can. In a town that has given so many men to the Fleet they know what war means.

Packing wool for dispatch to willing knitters.

Weary and footsore soldiers will thank you again and again for these.

1162/1163/1164/1165/1166/1167 A facsimile page from the *Daily Sketch*, Friday 28 August 1914, depicting war associated activity around Portsmouth. The captions are as they appeared beneath the original photographs. The identity numbers run from the top, left to right.

1203 Swansea women whose husbands and sons are on active service queuing to register for army pay. Note the shawls and flat caps.

1204 Bradford Boy Scouts mustered to raise money for the Prince of Wales's Relief Fund, 15 August 1914.

1207 Two German boys 'dressed to kill' were photographed at a review of German troops held by the Kaiser at Potsdam, August 1914.

1209 In Berlin men and women exchanging their gold wedding rings for iron ones engraved with 'Wilhelm II' so as to contribute to the War Fund.

1210 Dressed as a Death's Head Hussars is Princess Victoria Louise, Duchess of Brunswick, the Kaiser's only daughter. The Crown Princess is on the right.

1212 Kaiser Wilhelm II. (Frederick William Victor Albert.)

1211 Crown Prince Frederick William Victor Augustus Ernest Frederick.

1214 French reservists pouring out of the Gare du Nord railway terminus, Paris, on their way to their respective depots.

1213 Fervant patriotism in Petrograd: an emotional crowd led by a monk carrying a portait of the Czar, petition God to give Mother Russia the victory. *All alike feel that this war is a great, popular, liberating work which starts a new epoch in the history of the world,* commented Russian writer Professor Peter Struve, editor of 'Russian Thought'. *German aggression has united the whole population of Russia.* The slogan on the banner carried by the woman on the right reads: 'The Victory of Russia and Slavdom'.

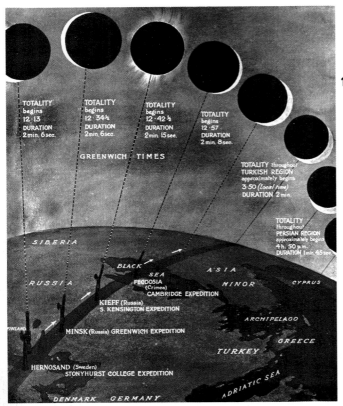

1208 As the Great War got underway and the slaughter began a solar eclipse that took place on Friday 21 August 1914, had the potential to cause terror and panic as the line of totality crossed over massed Russian armies awaiting to do battle with the Germans.

The Sphere magazine artist produced the graphics (left). The caption reads: *Owing to the great European war the arrangements of the various scientific expeditions to view the eclipse of the sun have been so seriously hampered that most of the expeditions have been cancelled altogether. In Russia the Czar and military authorities strove hard to spread the news of the eclipse so that the darkening of the sun during part of the day should not cause the illiterate Russian soldiers to believe that it was a bad omen.*

The phenomenon of the appearance of both sun and moon to be exactly the same size to observers on earth remained without comment; as did the mathematical precision and timing associated with the natural spectacle.

Chapter Three: **The Almighty's Choice – Which Side to Favour?**

906 A German pastor helps to settle any doubts in the hearts of his flock: divine favour rests with the Central Powers. God is certainly with Germany.

907 Archbishop of York, Cosmo Gordon Lang, visited The Grand Fleet where he addressed 1,600 officers and men of a destroyer flotilla. God obviously favours the British.

910 A service of intercession was held at Westminster Abbey, 23 August 1914. The gathering prayed for the success of the allied armies. The King and Queen are seen here leaving the Abbey.

912 The Bishop of London, Dr Winnington-Ingram in his war kit.

909 Pope Pius X died 20 August 1914 as the Great War broke out.

913 Pope Benedict XV, officially, took a neutral stand and offended millions of communicants on both sides.

916 German Army belt buckle with the words 'Gott Mit Uns' – God is With Us.

914/911 The Bishop of London conducts a drum-head service for London Territorials in front of St Pauls' Cathedral.

917 'Great is the God of the Russian Land' the Emperor of Russia, Czar Nicholas II holds a sacred icon before his kneeling soldiers who are told 'In prayer we call God's blessing on Holy Russia and her valiant troops'.

908 German Army Church Parade held behind the lines on the Western Front.

921 A French soldier priest officiates for his comrades.

920 A priest with the Belgian forces. He worked at tending wounded.

918 This Belgian priest, Rev J. Chanderlon of Antwerp, carries a cavalry sabre. The fact that this clergyman openly bore arms was a puzzle for the original caption writer at the time.

919 The Church and the war: London Territorials at St Pancras Church, where they deposited their Colours. The Colours, or banner which bore the battle honours of a particular battalion, were no longer carried into battle (the British Army's official last use was Majuba Hill, South Africa in 1881). 'Fear God and defend your country' were the words of Princess Louise at a Sunday service for London Territorials.

922 The Bishop of Birmingham, Dr Russell Wakefield, conducting a service at The White City stadium, London. The 17th Service Battalion of the Middlesex Regiment was a Kitchener battalion of the Middlesex Regiment, part of the British Army formed as a Pals battalion.

923 A Roman Catholic priest conducting a Mass in a stone quarry in northern France.

924 A Roman Catholic priest gives the benediction to recruits at the Military Academy in Vienna.

926 A German motor altar. The Archbishop of Cologne is on the left.

925 Roman Catholic Divine service conducted for French troops.

924 Russian Orthodox Church leaders in Pettrograd preside over celebrations for victories in battle.

928 Russian priest blessing a field gun. Now will its shells hit their target with more lethal accuracy?

932 Russian officers lining up to kiss a religious icon before going into battle.

933 Russian soldiers do not get to kiss the icon but are able to gaze at it from afar.

929 Germans attending Church Parade in occupied France.

934 Soldiers of the Roman Catholic faith at an open air service at Sittingbourne.

931 Battlefield damage to a calvary leaving the image intact. Yet another omen for the superstitious?

935 Lieutenant Colonel Fox and his company listen to speeches before entraining to Rotherham and the Territorial HQ of the York and Lancaster Regiment.

937 The Sultan of Turkey, Mehmed V, leaving the Mosque after the declaration of War on the allies.

938 The Sheikh-ul-Islam proclaiming a Holy War, Jihad, against Russian, French and British in November 1914.

935 Market Hill, Barnsley, 6 August 1914, town's dignitaries give the 'Terriers' of the 5th Battalion, York and Lancs, a civic send-off. Mayor, William Goodworth England, wishes the men 'God speed'; Church of England vicar, Reverend Richard Huggard, places God's stamp of approval on the proceedings as he punches the air with the rest of them.

939 Russian troops attending a religious service before marching to the Front.

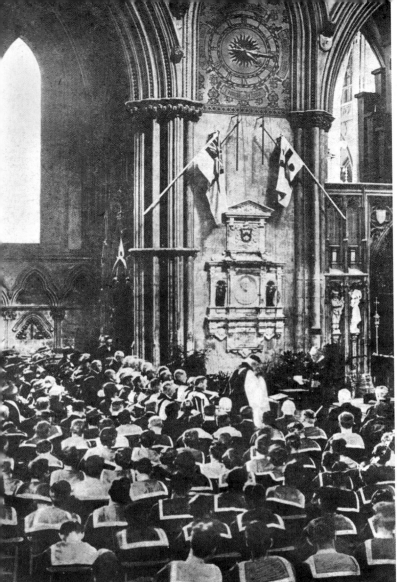

943 Professor Pares, authorized British correspondent at the Russian headquarters wrote: *An infantry regiment stood drawn up under arms and in a hollow square. A priest was preaching arrayed in rich blue vestments, he was saying, "Never forget that wherever you are and whatever is happening to you the eye of God is on you and watching over you". The priest placed a Bible bound in blue velvet on an improvised lectern of six bayonets and when turning to all sides he waved a crucifix at them.*

940 Unveiling ceremony at York Minster by Lord Zetland. Admiral Sir F. Bridgman is seen committing the memorial to the custody of the Dean of the Chapter. It is in memory of Admiral Cradock's officers and crew lost in the Battle of the Coronel Sea, 1 November 1914. Such-like memorials to those lost in battle would begin to appear in churches all over England as the war progressed.

944 French soldier-priest celebrating Mass at an army camp behind the front. There were no chaplains in the French army and priests were conscripted as soldiers. In 1914 some 22,000 priests were serving as soldiers.

942 With unquestioning faith in God and his Czar: Russian officers line up to kiss a cross and receive a blessing from an Eastern Orthodox cleryman before departing for the Front. Mothers, sisters, wives, children and sweethearts look on no doubt believing that the religious act will protect them.

945 German troops holding divine service accompanied by a brass band.

951 A Church of England clergyman conducting Holy Communion in South West Africa. Thus the idea is reinforced that God is 'batting' for the British. The original caption commented that, 'The clergy have been unflinching and untiring in their work and have faced danger without thought of self'.

952 First clergyman to be awarded the Distinguished Service Order, the Reverend Percy W. Guinness received the award when serving as Chaplain with the 16th Lancers, at Kruistraat, Belgium.

941 A religious thanksgiving service for their army's victory in battle, 1914, in the fighting in Northern France. Crowds gathered in Berlin at the Bismarck memorial.

948 Church of England chaplains conducting a military funeral for three British soldiers abroad.

946 A French soldier-priest says Mass for his comrades using a make-shift altar and items for the ceremony borrowed from a nearby church.

950 The Bishop of London holding a service in the camp of The London Rifle Brigade.

947 A Catholic priest saying Mass on one of the Mess decks aboard a British battleship.

930 A field service for German Jews held behind the line in France.

Chapter Four: Coming to Blows – August 1914

002 German infantry advancing into Belgium in August 1914. Thirty miles a day had to be achieved by soldiers of the First Army to conform to the Schlieffen Plan.

003 Belgian cavalry, part of a 288 strong force, about to attack the enemy 1,000 yards away. Machine-gun fire wiped most of them out.

003 The German plan was to defeat France in forty-two days, then move its armies by rail to take on the Russians. Here a train arrives in Belgium with mounted guards.

004 Belgian infantry on the march. On the right a Belgian priest can be seen wearing a Red Cross band.

007 German infantry in Belgium in the summer of 1914.

009 Prussian Cuirassiers entering Mouland, near Visé, on the way to attack the Belgian town of Liége. They are carrying ten foot long lances.

006 Captured German equipment being taken to the capitol, Brussels, for display as spoils of war.

008 Getting in the harvest and preparing to meet the invaders carries on side by side.

010 Belgian infantry man a simple road block on the Waelhem road leading to the port of Antwerp.

011 A fleet of armoured cars used by the Belgians to take on the German mounted troops.

012 Exhausted Belgian soldiers resting following an action.

121/121a A flimsy road block manned by Belgian infantry.

013 German Cuirassiers and Uhlans watering their horses in at a village trough.

014 Belgian soldier contacts headquarters using the latest technology – a field telephone.

016 German cavalrymen having their wounds dressed following action on the approaches to Liége.

017 Belgian machine gun team preparing a defensive position in a beet field.

018 German supply column following up the advance on Brussels passes through the shell damaged Belgian village of Visé.

019 Belgian priest on his way to administer some religious consolation to the wounded and dying. He is accompanied by a Belgian medical officer.

021 A Sister of Mercy carrying water to an advanced Belgian outpost at Haelen, close to the German positions.

023 German infantry massed together in line during their advance across the Belgian countryside.

020 German supply wagon delivering a load of fodder for the mounted troops' horses.

022 German artillery battery in a firing position.

024 The road from Tirlemont to Brussels thronged with fleeing refugees; among them are many priests and Red Cross workers.

025 A German camp outside the town of Visé. A group of captured Belgian soldiers can be seen in the hollow ground. In the forefront a group of civilian spectators observe the scene.

026 Inside the German camp at Visé.

028 The streets of Brussels packed with Belgian troops gathered to repel the invaders.

029 Belgian troops marching out to do battle.

031 Exhausted Belgian infantry and their dogs harnessed to pull a machine gun.

118 German infantry in camp at Charleroi being served with soup which is being doled out into the men's mess tins.

030 A Belgian officer receives treatment for a slight wound.

032 Belgian soldiers quartered in a church near Louvain.

033 A troop of Belgian Lancers riding through the streets of Louvain.

034 Belgian Civic Guard with dogs pulling machine guns, falling back on Antwerp.

036 A Section of Belgian dog handlers. Dogs were used to draw small light carts loaded with weapons, ammunition and other supplies.

038 Belgian women filling the water bottles of the invading Germans. There would be many who would disapprove.

035 Belgian infantrymen in action near Louvain, 20 August.

037 Germans using captured Belgian dogs to pull their cart.

039 Belgian refugees resting beside the road during their flight towards Ghent.

040 The 2nd Battalion Grenadier Guards leaving Chelsea Barracks for the fighting in Belgium and France. Queen Alexandra is there to watch them go.

040a Sir John French was appointed to command the BEF.

070 The Kaiser called the BEF 'Contemptible'; here some of these are seen boarding a transport at Southampton.

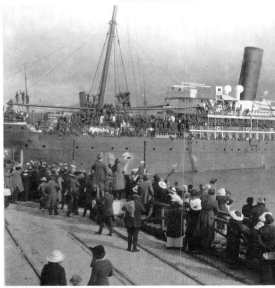

071 Men of the British Expeditionary Force leaving for France receive a joyful send-off.

044 'Are we downhearted?' a 'No!' for the cameraman.

043 British 'Tommies' bound for France. Snatching 40-winks during the Channel crossing

046 British cavalry on the quay at Boulogne. On their arrival British soldiers were fêted by the townspeople and invited to take what they wanted from some of the shops gratis.

045 A battalion of a Scottish regiment march off the quayside after arriving at Boulogne.

047 A Royal Artillery column at Boulogne after being landed at the Loubet Dock, 18 August 1914, makes its way to prepared quarters.

049 British Royal Navy Marines arriving at Ostend 27 August and seen here marching to take up positions to stop the invaders.

048 A British Army transport fleet.

053 A British transport section on the docks at Boulogne.

050 The City of London Rough Riders with their machine gun strapped to a horse. In addition to carrying a machine gun the horse would have been harnessed to an ammunition or forage cart.

054 Royal Marines resting near outside the town of Ostend.

051 German troops during a period of rest on during their advance into Belgium.

052 German troops at their ease and enjoying a drink. Water was doled out twice a day during the war of movement.

055 The German Emperor, Kaiser Wilhelm, with some of his generals.

056 Avenue de Maestrict in the Belgian town of Visé. One of the early towns captured by the Germans.

058 Handing out rations.

059 German 17-inch (42cm) howitzer.

062 Belgian fort after bombardment and capture.

061a A Belgian fort gun cupola before the fighting began.

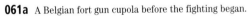

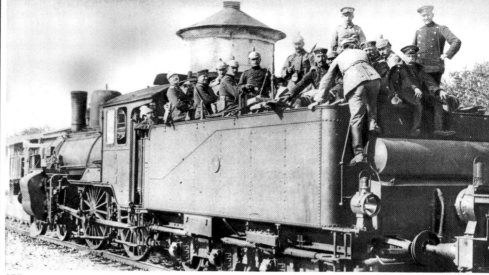

057 The German rail network was to transport troops to the fighting in Russia; however, the matter of a quick French defeat had not happened. Consequently railway timetables were behind.

061 German howitzer in firing position.

063 Steel and concrete gun position smashed to rubble by German guns.

064 Belgians defending Antwerp.

065 Germans advancing on Antwerp.

067 British soldiers of the Royal Naval Division march out to take up positions for the defence of the vital port of Antwerp.

068 'Blue Jackets' of the Royal Naval Division ready to repel the invaders.

066 German General von Beseler who led the successful attack on Antwerp.

069 A Belgian rearguard defending a canal bridge as the main force falls back to Antwerp.

072 Belgians manning a defence line at Antwerp.

042/041 The Germans adopted a policy of intimidation against the people of occupied territory to discourage acts of resistance. Belgians are being searched and could be accused of being *franc-tireurs* and shot. Justification: German war artist, 'Felix', depicted a civilian firing on German troops.

073 Germans on the approaches to Antwerp.

DEFENCES OF ANTWERP

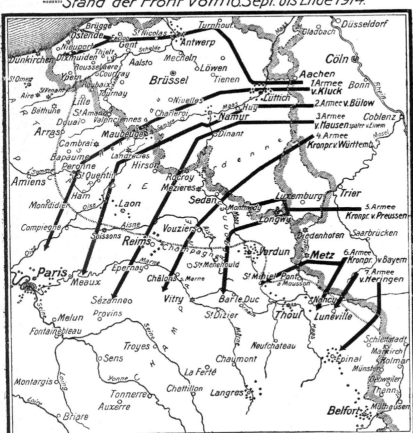

Vorstoss der Deutschen Armeen im Aug. u. Sept. 1914

Stand der Front vom 16. Sept. bis Ende 1914.

0   25   50   75   100 Klm.

074 Antwerp defence system included an area of countryside that could be flooded by opening sluices on the banks of the River Scheldt.

The port of Antwerp was designated as the National Redoubt and consisted of four defensive lines:

1. A ring of 21 forts approximately 10 to 15 km outside the city.
2. A secondary line of resistance of twelve older forts around 5 km outside to the city.
3. A group of two forts and three coastal batteries defending the river Scheldt.
4. Pre-prepared areas that could be flooded.

King Albert, king of the Belgians, led his army through the Siege of Antwerp and held the Germans off long enough for Britain and France to prepare for the Battle of the Marne (6 to 9 September 1914).

075 Belgian soldiers landing at Ostend, 30 August 1914, to defend the port against the approaching enemy.

076 Overcome by panic as the Germans begin to bombard Antwerp these people crowd the quays in an effort to get away from the city.

077 The last refugee tug from Antwerp: a baby is handed down to its mother.

079/079a Near panic on the gangplank as the boats to England and safety fill up. The above scenes took place at Ostend. Note the Marine with rifle blocking the gangplank. Belgian cyclist troops with their machines embark to be landed at Calais.

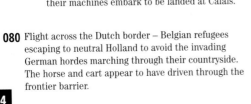

080 Flight across the Dutch border – Belgian refugees escaping to neutral Holland to avoid the invading German hordes marching through their countryside. The horse and cart appear to have driven through the frontier barrier.

078 Near panic on the gangplank as the boats to England and safety fill up.

082 German infantry celebrate after capturing a Belgian gun.

081 German infantry on the outskirts of Antwerp pause before a destroyed church.

084 German infantry take cover behind a make-shift barricade on the approaches to Antwerp.

086 Lieutenant General Deguise the Belgian commander of Antwerp.

087 A barbed wire barricade running through the streets of Antwerp. Note the children and other civilians not yet evacuated from this defence line.

083 Wreckage of five Belgian locomotives sent together at full speed to block the lines. The Germans were bringing up troops to the fighting from their base at Malines by rail and this method was devised to disrupt the reinforcement of the attackers.

085 Royal Navy Bluejackets in position alongside the Belgian defenders of Antwerp.

088 The removal of the Belgian Government to France. Official records and books being carted away from Antwerp. A proclamation declared: *'It is important that the Belgian Government should provisionally establish its seat in a location where it can assure the continuity of the national sovereignty.'* By invitation from the French Government Belgian administration was set up at the French port of Le Havre.

089 Some Marines of the 63rd (Royal Naval Division) who were among the defenders of Antwerp. Judging from their appearance they may have just come out of the defensive lines drawn around Antwerp.

090 Some 'Bluejackets' from the same division, kitted in full scale marching order with great packs, fill their water bottles from containers brought up by Belgian children. The marked contrast with their comrades pictured above may be noted.

091 The Belgian capital, Brussels, was occupied by the Germans 20 August 1914. Here jack-booted infantry march through Pace Charles Rogier watched by silent crowds. The Belgian Government had fled to Antwerp before going on to Le Havre in France.

092 Thursday morning 20 August 50,000 German troops entered Brussels.

093 Adolphe Eugène Henri Max, Burgomaster of Brussels. He met the invaders outside the city to inform them officially it was undefended. He refused to cooperate with them and was imprisoned.

094a German troops on a street in Brussels.

097a Companies of infantry and artillery in the Grand Place Brussels. German lancers are arriving in the square.

094b German officers in Brussels. The occupying troops behaved well and paid for their food and drink.

094 German Red Cross men with a captured Belgian war dog.

096 German soldiery trampling the flower beds in Brussels (according to one caption).

095 Germans with a commandeered cart and driver leaving Brussells to continue their advance into Belgium.

095/100 One of the gigantic Austrian siege guns used to smash the Belgian forts – two were used to destroy Antwerp fortifications. They were transported in sections so as to be able to cross road bridges.

101 Fort de Stabroeck, one of the outer defence forts guarding Antwerp. When it was in danger of being captured intact Belgian engineers blew it up.

103 A Zeppelin leaves its base at Friedrichshafen on Lake Constance for a sorté against the Allies.

105 Grim-faced Belgian soldiers photographed against a house damaged by a Zeppelin bomb.

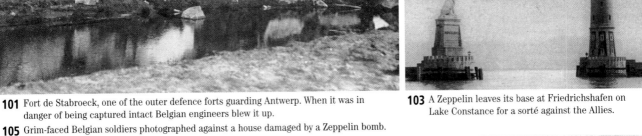

104 The results of a Zeppelin attack. A bomb exploded in Peid Public (street in Antwerp) killing five civilians and injuring ten. Note the Belgian Boy Scout surveying the damage.

102 Make-shift repairs after a Zeppelin attack.

106 Germany's latest Zeppelin at anchor on Lake Constance.

107 Panic on the streets of Antwerp as the Germans overcome the city's defences.

109 After destroying this bridge near Hamms the Belgian soldiers man a hastily thrown up barricade on the river bank.

108 German fire power came as a shock to the Allies as the German army employed Maxim machine guns in great number. Here, on the outskirts of Brussels, a Regiment's horse drawn machine guns are paraded.

110 A pause in the advance as a German officer surveys the ground ahead before issuing the order to continue.

111 Drastic times call for drastic measures; a gate arch on the approaches to the city of Antwerp is being dismantled to give an uninterrupted field of fire to the guns of the defending artillery.

112 King Albert, king of the Belgians, stands in the gateway close to the firing line. He set an example for his troops as his kingdom continued to shrink under the jackboots of the invaders.

113 A series of four photographs showing a Belgian field gun team bringing their Krupps manufactured weapon into action.

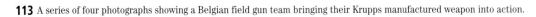

114 The order is given to evacuate Antwerp and a fleet of London buses can be seen lined up to take elements of the Royal Naval Division to Ostend.

115 The bridge of boats over the River Scheldt; one route to safety in neutral Holland.

116 Belgian families arriving at Dover Harbour in a fishing smack.

117 German marines entering Antwerp after the evacuation of the city 9 October 1914.

123 German marines survey hastily abandoned clothing and equipment on a quayside in Antwerp.

124 Some Royal Navy Bluejackets heading for the port of Ostend after withdrawing from Antwerp.

125 A London omnibus under new management; abandoned by the BEF at Antwerp.

127 The British found London buses useful for transporting troops; D219 is seen here being used by the Germans.

126 Admiral von Schroeder German Governor of Antwerp after its capture.

129 Decorations followed the German victory.

128 A German military band plays at a ceremony in the main square at Antwerp.

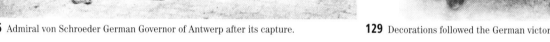

130 Dutch soldiers behind a barrier of barbed wire and revolving spike at a Belgium-Holland border crossing point.

133 The original caption in the *War Budget* magazine says: During the retreat from Antwerp a section of the British Naval Brigade marched accidently into Holland and were compelled by international law to lay down their arms. It goes on to say that they will be interned for the rest of the war. From Antwerp, 1,500 sailors of the division fled to the neutral Netherlands, where they were interned. Units of the Royal Naval Division that managed to withdraw from Antwerp returned to England, arriving 11 October 1914. Approximately, a further 1,000 men of the RND were captured by the Germans.

131 Men of the 63rd (Royal Naval) Division under escort of Dutch guards.

132 An RND internee makes friends.

134 RND internees in the market place at Leeuwarden examine the local produce.

135 Two Royal Marines retreating from Antwerp along with soldiers of the Belgian army.

136 Belgian cavalry evacuating the town of Ghent.

137 A section of Belgian artillery falling back towards Ostend.

138 Covering the retreat, a Belgian machine gunner operating a Maxim.

139 A Belgian machine gun manning a light machine gun.

141 Short rest for food during the German advance.

140a Relentless march through Belgium.

140 A roadside break.
037 German Uhlans scouting the way ahead.

142 Continuing success although Belgian resistance was slowing forward momentum.

143a Next stop Paris?

143 Some slightly wounded.

144 German medical corps dogs used for locating the wounded.

145 German advance guard arrive at the Hotel de Ville, Ghent, 14 October 1914.

149 A supplement to army rations – fresh milk.

146 Bottles of mineral water for the thirsty invaders.

147 Battle weary German infantry seen here bringing in a wounded comrade on a broken section of a ladder, which serves as a make-shift stretcher.

161 German Marines taking a herd in for milking. To the victor the spoil.

152 In the main square at Antwerp after its capture.

154 Belgian prisoners of war, happy to be alive, in the main square at Antwerp.

162 German officers sample the food of a field kitchen operating in the streets of a Belgian town.

163 Proud German Marine guard.

157 Infantry paraded to listen to orders for a forthcoming attack.

151 A mid-day rest during the German advance.

150 Captured Belgian war dogs brought into service for the Germans to draw machine guns and ammunition supplies.

153/155 Belgian Lancers set up and man a road block in the path of the German advance.

159 The Belgian coast is reached by the Germans and they dig in.

166 A funeral parade in Belgium complete with brass band.

165 A German padre reads the burial service for a fallen soldier.

164 The Belgian coast resort of Blankenberghe receives unwelcome visitors.

164a Opportunity to paddle at Blankenberghe.

159 Germans among the sand dunes.
160 German Maxim machine guns on makeshift wooden rigs for defence against air attacks.

167 Royal Flying Corps FE2 B.

170 Royal Flying Corps FE2 B was a main aircraft during the early part of the war.

173 Royal Flying Corps FE2 B showing armament which in this instance consists of three Lewis guns.

174 German machine gun team using an armoured plate protection shield.
176 Among the dunes medical officers render first aid to a casualty.

175 Belgians among the sand dunes near Dixmude.

177 A Belgian nurse exchanges banter with a Belgian soldier. Likely he is attempting to persuade her to do his laundry.

178 A captured German officer salutes the Belgian regimental colours being carried folded and held by the standard bearer. An odd ritual of war.

180/181 Belgian soldiers manning very shallow trenches. Within weeks trenches doubled in depth. These would barely suffice as protection.

179 A Belgian infantry battalion rests on the sands behind trenches constructed in the dunes.

182 A Belgian in the dunes.

183 Albert, King of the Belgians, an inspiration to his fighting men is seen here near Nieuport. He is to the left, at the front of the vehicle discussing matters with the small officer.

184 Belgian Hussars resting outside a church.

Chapter Five: Into the Fray – British at Mons

185 German infantry waiting for the order to advance.

186 British cavalry advancing through a Belgian village, August 1914.

187 From Aldershot to active service; 1st Battalion Black Watch march to the station. They would be involved at Mons.

192 General Sir Douglas Haig, commanding I Corps.

189 A Royal Flying Corps RE 5 two-seater being landed in France.

188 His Majesty's Transport Rowan More arriving at Boulogne with troops of the BEF.

195 Lieutenant General Sir William Pulteney, commanding III Corps.

194 Major General Sir Edmund H. H. Allenby, commanding Cavalry.

198 British transport at Boulogne. 40,000 horses went to France with the BEF.

190 British soldiers crowd the decks of a troop ship as it approaches the harbour.

193 General Sir H. L. Smith-Dorrien, commanding II Corps.

196 A horse that would not tackle the gangway being slung ashore.

197 Some German prisoners for the return trip across the Channel.

191 British nurses arriving at Dieppe in August 1914.

206 'Bonjour mademoiselle!' The British Tommies arrive in France.

207 British Tommies enjoying a drink with their French comrades.

208 British troops about to leave their last tented camp to march into Belgium to attempt to throw back the invading German army. Their first contact with the enemy would be at the town of Mons.

201 Men of the 2nd Battalion, Seaforth Highlanders crossing a canal in Belgium on their way to Mons.

203 Marching through French countryside, men of the 1st Battalion, Leicestershire Regiment head towards the Belgian border and Mons.

202 Despatch riders with a London Regiment pose for a photograph in the square at Merville, France, August 1914. The motorbikes are B.S.A.500cc machines circ 1912.

205 British infantry take a meal on the way to Mons.

209 Gifts of fruit and flowers from a grateful French people.

210 British infantry winning hearts among some French children.

200 British infantry in a French town on the way to Mons in Belgium.

199 Cavalry on its way to meet the advancing Germans.

212 British artillery transported on the French railway system.

211 British artillery in a French town on the way to Mons in Belgium.

213 Cavalry acting as scouts at the vanguard of the British Army marching on Mons.

214 A view from the church tower looking along the Mons-Condé canal. The railway station is in the foreground.

214a The main street and church belfry at Mons.
214 View from the church tower over Mons old quarter.
215 A cavalry scout keeps watch.
217 The 1st Battalion Cameron Highlanders before Mons.

218 August 21, 1914 and the British advance guard enters Mons.

219 Two scouts attempting to gain information from the locals. Language was a barrier.

221 Civilians assist the British soldiers to erect barricades in the streets.

223 Tommies in the streets of Mons.

220 Men resting at the village of Jemappes, Mons, 22 August.

224 Main square at Mons, 22 August: 4th Battalion The Royal Fusiliers. The following day they took positions north of the town at Nimy holding a line behind the Mons-Condé canal. Two of their number, Private Sidney Godley and Captain James Dease, were to win the first Victoria Crosses of the First World War.

225 August 22: Private Carter, 4th Battalion The Middlesex Regiment on guard at Mons. On the 23rd this battalion was involved in a heavy engagement at Obourg, to the east of Mons.

222 Defences in the form of slit trenches at Mons.

226 Vickers machine gun section transporting their weapon and boxes of ammunition on mules.

230 British soldiers fixing a machine gun in position.

231 Royal Artillery men with their 13 pounder await the enemy attack.

232 German soldiers in the square at the Belgian town of Bruges, August 1914.　**233** German artillery moving up in Belgium.

236 German artillery horses bringing 77mm field guns into action.

235 German artillerymen bringing a 77mm field gun into a firing position.

237 In touch with the OP.   **234** Hauling a 120mm heavy Krupp Howitzer into place.

238 Bavarians with bayonets fixed and looking ready for the attack.

246 Royal Engineers despatch riders acting as scouts tasked with locating the advancing Germans.

241 British soldiers working at Mons, preparing for the coming fight.

239 German infantry awaiting the order to advance.

240 A snapshot taken by a British soldier: infantry in a position of defence on a bridge at Mons.

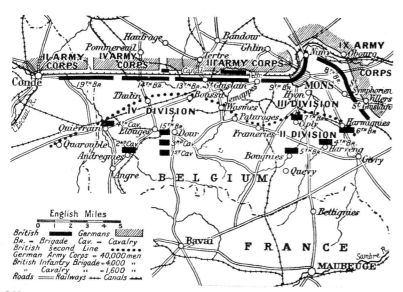

242 British positions along the Conde-Mons canal stalling the German advance.

244 A horde of grey-clad figures began overwhelming the British defence line.

243 British positions along the Conde-Mons canal stalling the German advance.

228 The German army's method of attack in 1914 was by employing massed ranks. This was portrayed by a German artist as a glorious event as depicted here.

247 British infantry in 1914 operating a machine gun.

227 British infantry at Mons firing fifteen or more aimed rounds a minute made an impression on the packed attackers.

249 The result of attacking in massed ranks was that the attacking soldiers were killed and fell in ranks.

250 The Germans capture Mons.

251 British officers planning the retreat from Mons.

252 British infantry taking a break for a bite and a brew during the withdrawal from Mons.

253 British cavalry on the run at a gallop.

254 Men of the 1st Battalion, Cameronians (Scottish Rifles) taking a rest during the retreat.

256 Elements of British cavalry keeping ahead of the advancing Germans who are intent on capturing the French capitol.

255 German artillery moving through a French village during the advance towards Paris.

257 Commanding officer of the 1st Battalion The Cameronians, Lieutenant Colonel Robertson, looking for signs of the pursuing enemy.

258 Marching in good order this Highland battalion shows they have not being routed.

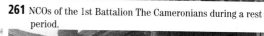

261 NCOs of the 1st Battalion The Cameronians during a rest period.

259 Cavalry scouting the retreat route.

260 The retreat is still underway and on the 29 August the camera captures 1st Battalion The Cameronians at their breakfast.

263 British infantry resting by a French canal.

262 German artillery battery men with their 7.7cm field gun.

266 German cavalry, men and horses, brought down by British rear guard.

267 German battery about to open fire.

264 Under fire: an air burst rains shrapnel and, as the picture is taken, the despatch rider, centre, receives a wound to the head.

265 German cavalry keep up the pressure on the retreating French and British.

268 British 13pdr gun crew during the retreat from Mons.

270 Néry: In this Matania painting Captain Bradbury, Sergeant Major Dorrell and Sergeant Nelson are depicted operating F Gun during the fighting.

269 British 13pdr gun crew, men and horses killed in battle.

271 Men of L Battery, Royal Horse Artillery, before leaving for France, 1914.

274 Lt M.J. Deace VC, Royal Fusiliers, for action at Mons. Died of wounds.

275 Pte S.F. Godley VC, Royal Fusiliers, for action at Mons.

276 Capt E.K. Bradbury VC, Royal Horse Artillery, for action at Néry.

273 Sgt Maj G. Dorrell VC, Royal Horse Artillery, for action at Néry.

272 Sgt D. Nelson VC, Royal Horse Artillery, for action at Néry.

282 After the destruction of the British guns of L Battery at Néry the British cavalry counter-attacked driving the Germans back. Here men of the 2nd Dragoon Guards (Queen's Bays) have just captured some prisoners.

288 A captured horse belonging to the 9th Uhlans is inspected by a British officer. The *9th Pommersches Ulanen* were on the right flank of the German attack at Néry.

278 German Uhlans arrive in the French town of Doullens, Somme, in September 1914 at 11.30. They are returning after having checked that the town is clear of French troops. Towns people follow the invaders through the main street. A French photographer captures the moment. His other photographs are taken secretly from an upstairs room over the shop.

The Great War Illustrated in Colour
August to December 1914

German infantry being transported to the newly formed trench lines stretching across France and Belgium from the Channel to the borders of Switzerland.   Coloured by Jon Wilkinson

Co05 Kaiser Frederick William Victor Albert of Prussia.

Co05 Emperor Franz Joseph Emperor of Austria; Apostolic King of Hungary; King of Bohemia; King of Croatia; King of Galicia and Lodomeria; Grand Duke of Cracow.

Co04 George V (George Frederick Ernest Albert; 3 June 1865 – 20 January 1936) was King of the United Kingdom and the British Dominions, and Emperor of India.

Co02 Nikolay II, Nikolay Alexandrovich Romanov, Emperor and Autocrat of All the Russias.

Co10 Albert I reigned as King of the Belgians.

Great Britain does not want a single nation dominating europe (just across the Channel) and makes friendship deal with Russia and France – **The Triple Entente**

Russia eyes Germany and Austro Hungary with suspicion and befriends France and Great Britain thus isolating and surrounding her enemy's borders – **The Triple Entente** Meanwhile she keeps her eye on Japan

The United States is keeping out of involvement in Europe

France feels threatened by Germany and has a friendships with Britain and Russia – **The Triple Entente**

Italy contracts to come to the aide of Austro Hungary and Germany should their sovereignty come under threat – **The Triple Alliance**

Germany feels threatened with likely foes on both her frontiers. Hence **The Triple Alliance**

Turkey – the old Ottoman empire is in decline and keeps out of it

Co11 Sultan Mehmed V Reshad, Turkey.

Co07 Victor Emmanuel III King of the Italians.

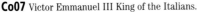

Co08 Raymond Poincaré, President of France.

Co09 Peter I King of the Serbs, Croats and Slovenes.

Faced with the possibility of having to wage war on two fronts – because of the Triple Entente entered into by France, Britain and Russia – the German Army Chief of Staff, Alfred von Schlieffen, was asked to plan a way of preventing this. His initial plan was produced in 1905: he believed that it was a priority to defeat France first and quickly, force that nation to surrender before Russia had a chance to mobilize. Then, using the German railway system, move the bulk of the army to the east to defeat the Russians. The plan required the Germans to pass through Belgium on the way to engage the French army.

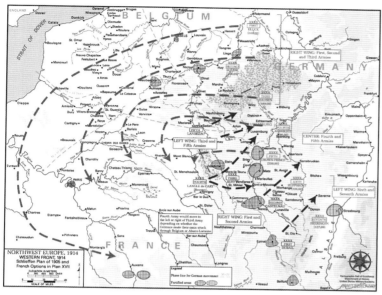

Co13 The entire plan was based upon the following assumptions: Russia would take at least six weeks to mobilize; France would be defeated in six weeks; Belgium would not resist the German army passing through its territory and that Britain would remain neutral. These assumptions were seriously mistaken. Also note from the plan above, the right wing of the sweeping movement was intended to pass the west of Paris. That did not happen as the commanders on the German right flank felt isolated and tended to draw in, passing to the east of Paris and so failing to encircle the French capital and bring about its fall.

Co14 Alfred von Schlieffen. He died on 4 January, 1913, just 19 months before the outbreak of The Great War. His last words are said to have been, 'Remember: keep the right wing very strong'. Nonconformance to this directive in August 1914 was one cause of the Plan's failure.

The european kings and emperors were itching for a fight and an excuse was needed to justify their beligerent intent. It came on the 28 June when the heir of the Austria-Hungarian throne and his wife were shot dead on the streets of Sarajevo.

Co17 Archduke Franz Ferdinand and his consort Sophie, Duchess of Hohenberg, about to set off for the fatal drive through the streets of Serajevo, the capitol of Bosnia and Herzegovina.

o15 Nedjelko Cabrinoviç threw a bomb at the Archduke's car but it was warded off by the Archduke himself. The bomb fell in the road near a following vehicle in the motorcade wounding the occupants.

Co16 Gavrillo Princip was suddenly confronted by the open-topped car when it took a wrong turn. While reversing the driver stalled the engine. Princip fired on the royal couple killing them both.

Coloured by Jon Wilkinson

Co18 Men of Regiment 47, *Fifth Armee,* advancing through the Ardenne in August 1914. Coloured by Jon Wilkinson

Co19 German infantry during the advance in to Belgium and Luxembourg, August 1914.

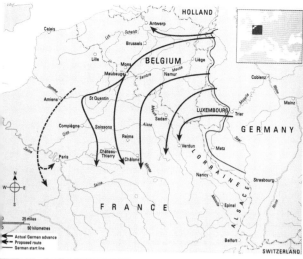

Co21 German artillery rolling into Belgium 1914.

Co23 How the German invasion plan failed to surround and capture Paris.

Co116 Lieutenant-General Sir Aylmer Hunter-Weston commanded of 11 Infantry Brigade this unit as part of 4th Division in the BEF was involved at the battles of Le Cateau and the Aisne.

Co23 German Uhlans at a pre-war parade original caption: 'The Terrible Uhlans'.

Co24 The Belgian army put up a stiff resistance against overwhelming odds and by so doing interfered with the German plan to defeat France in six weeks.

1914

5

Co25 German Uhlans pause to water their horses in Belgian village, 1914 .

Co26 German artillery rolling through the French countryside, 1914.

Co27 German howitzer crews manning their Skoda 149 mm guns during the opening moves in 1914. *Coloured by Jon Wilkinson*

Co28 The German 77 mm field gun, Model 96, designed and built by the Krupp organization. It was the principal German field gun at the outbreak of the First World War and over 5,000 were still in service when the war ended. The calibre of 77 mm was chosen so that captured guns could not be re-bored to fire Allied standard ammunition, which was 75 mm or 76.2 mm. However, captured British and French pieces could have their barrels re-bored to fire German ammunition.

Coloured by Jon Wilkinson

Coloured by Jon Wilkinson

Co29 A German field artillery unit passing through a French town in 1914.　　**Co30** Hauling a 77 mm field gun into a position to lay down a barrage.

Coloured by Jon Wilkinson

Co31 Another French town is on fire and German soldiers are in the streets with French civilians looking on helplessly.

Coloured by Jon Wilkinson

Co34 The riverside at Namur with barges sunk into the mud of the River Meuse.

Co35 Victorious Germans Parade in the Grande Place, Lille.

Co37 Border town of Visé on the River Meuse, one of the first towns to be invaded by the German Army in 1914.

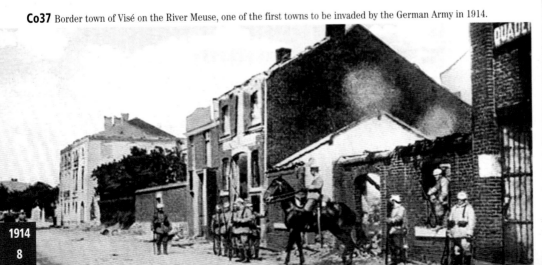

Co32 A German camera captures the scene where fighting took place in the French town of Lille.

Coloured by
Jon Wilkinson

Co33 Mons: The bridge over the canal on the Rues des Bragnons. The bridge lifting gear is on the Maisieres side.

Co38 Cavalry are cheered on by peasants as they ride out to meet the invaders.

Co39 Civilians surveying shell damage to buildings. The novelty would become commonplace.

1914

9

Co44 French infantry providing a guard for the Army's spotter planes.

Co45 North African Turco troops captured by the Germans. Note the bright uniforms.

Co50 French infantry moving to take up new positions during the opening weeks of August.

Co52 Belgian troops moving a barricade aside to allow their French allies through.

Co46 Belgian guides arrive to assist the British Expeditionary Force.

Co47 A battery of the Belgian artillery equipped with the quick-firing French 75 mm field gun, take up a firing position on a country track.

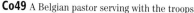

Co49 A Belgian pastor serving with the troops.

Co51 A battery of French 55 mm field guns in position on a reverse slope behind the River Marne.

Co53 French infantry practising the charge.

Co54 French cavalrymen at their ablutions.

Co55 Retreating Belgian soldiers escaping from Antwerp arrive at another port.

Co56 German infantry move with caution towards one of the Belgian forts wrecked by their bombardment. A ring of forts protected the city of Liege and were systematically smashed.

Coloured by Jon Wilkinson

Co58 These Belgian civilians are being marched off to be shot. They have been found guilty of shooting at the columns of German soldiers and of destroying bridges.

Coloured by Jon Wilkinson

Co41 Belgian infantry at a make-shift barricade await the hordes of German massed columns flooding through their countryside. Coloured by Jon Wilkinson

Co40 French infantry entered the fighting in 1914 dressed as if on ceremonial parade, with red kepi and red trousers. Easy targets for the grey-clad German riflemen. Coloured by Jon Wilkinson

Co43 German Uhlans passing through the streets of the French town of Doullens, August 1914. Coloured by Jon Wilkinson

Co42 German infantry take cover as they come under fire from defending forces. Coloured by Jon Wilkinson

Coloured by Jon Wilkinson

Co60 Officers of 1st Battalion East Lancashire Regiment taking a break during their rail journey to join the British Exeditionary Force near Le Cateau.

Co64 Men of the 4th Battalion Royal Fusiliers resting in the town square, Mons, 22 August. Their first defence position was the canal bank at Nimy.

Coloured by Jon Wilkinson

Co62 A regular battalion of the British Exeditionary Force on a forced march through Belgium. Coloured by Jon Wilkinson

Co63 Belgium, and British regulars waiting to put into use the high, aimed, rate of fire they had been practising for years.   Coloured by Jon Wilkinson

Co65 British infantry having just stopped German Uhlans.   Coloured by Jon Wilkinson

Co66 German infantry brought down in lines – the results of massed attack over open ground.   Coloured by Jon Wilkinson

Co61 British Exeditionary Force, Royal Artillery, near Le Cateau August 1914.   Coloured by Jon Wilkinson

Co67 The Great War saw the introduction of mass employment of the machine gun. Here a Vickers crew at their deadly work. The machine gun typically required a six to eight-man team: one to fire, one to feed the ammunition, the rest to help carry the weapon, its ammunition and spare parts.

Coloured by Jon Wilkinson

Co68 The German Army's *Maschinengewehr* 08, which was similar in design to the British Maxim and Vickers machine guns. Coloured by Jon Wilkinson

Co115 Helmuth Johann Ludwig von Moltke was Chief of the German General Staff at the outbreak of the Great War. His modification of the German attack plan to defeat France within six weeks and his inability to retain control of his rapidly advancing armies, especially the right flank, significantly contributed to the halt of the German offensive on the Marne in September 1914 and the frustration of German efforts for a rapid, decisive victory. Depressed, he stood down. In September 1914 the Kaiser had him replaced.

Co22 Eric von Falkenhayn succeeded Moltke as Chief of the General Staff of the German Army following the Battle of the Marne, 14 September 1914. Confronted with the failure of the Schlieffen Plan Falkenhayn attempted to outflank the British and French in the 'Race to the Sea', a series of engagements of quick movement throughout northern France and Belgium in which each side tried to turn the other's flank until they reached the coastline and stopped October – November 1914.

1914

Co69 Much of the fighting at Mons took place in built up areas from which many of the inhabitants had been unable to flee in time.

Coloured by Jon Wilkinson

Co70 Likely this photograph was taken during German Army pre-war manoeuvres.   Coloured by Jon Wilkinson

Co84 British cavalry advancing through a Belgian village, August 1914.   Coloured by Jon Wilkinson

Co71 German cavalry caught by British artillery attempting to cross the canal at Mons. Coloured by Jon Wilkinson

Co72 Lieutenant Colonel Robertson (smoking cigarette), commanding 1st Battalion, The Cameronians (Scottish Rifles) during a rest period for the battalion, along with some of his officers during the retreat from Mons, August 1914. Coloured by Jon Wilkinson

Co73 Artist impression of exhausted British cavalry during the retreat from Mons, August 1914. *Coloured by Jon Wilkinson*

Co74 Exhausted French dragoons snatch a quick sleep during the retreat. Note they have not removed their boots and are ready to mount and ride again when the order is given.

Co75 A German coloured postcard showing British and French prisoners being fed shortly after their capture. The photographer in his hand colouring has taken liberties with the tartan pattern on the Scots' kilts.

Co76 British and French prisoners are marched along the rue Faidherbe and through the Place du Théâtre in Lille.
Coloured by Jon Wilkinson

Co77 Original caption reads: French Cuiassiers helping a wounded comrade near St Quentin. Perhaps this was more a case of heat fatigue, as the style of uniform, including breastplates, dated from the Napoleonic period and was impractical for twentieth century warfare.

Co78 The Kaiser and General Hindenberg.

Co79 British prisoners taken at Mons by men of the German 24th Regiment, 12 Brigade, 6th Division. This German regiment had crossed into Belgium 12 August as part of General von Kluck's First Army.

Coloured by Jon Wilkinson

Co85 New recruits being sworn in with right hands placed on copies of the Bible. The four young men appear to have taken time off from their place of work to join the army. *I will be faithful and bear true Allegiance to His Majesty King George the Fifth, His Heirs, and Successors, and that I will, as in duty bound, honestly and faithfully defend His Majesty, His Heirs, and Successors, in Person, Crown, and Dignity against all enemies, and will observe and obey all orders of His Majesty, His Heirs, and Successors, and of the Generals and Officers set over me. So help me God.* So help them God indeed!   Coloured by Jon Wilkinson

Co83 Paul von Hindenburg, commanded the Eighth Army in 1914.

Coloured by Jon Wilkinson

Co80 General Alexander Heinrich Rudolph von Kluck, commanded the German First Army.

Co81 Kaiser Wilhelm II.
Coloured by Jon Wilkinson

Co82 General Erich Friedrich Wilhelm Ludendorff, in 1914 Deputy Chief of Staff to the German Second Army.

Coloured by Jon Wilkinson

Co87 SMS *Scharnhorst* engaged the *Good Hope* with her twelve 8.2-inch guns at a distance of seven miles.

Co86 Vice Admiral Maximilian Reichsgraf von Spee commanded the German East Asia Squadron and was based at Tsingtao within the German concession in China. In 1912 when he began his command the armored cruisers of his squadron were the newest in the German fleet. Within a few short years his ships became obsolete with the introduction of the battlecruiser. At the Battle of Coronel off the coast of Chile on 1 November 1914, Spee's force engaged and sank two British armored cruisers commanded by Sir Christopher Cradock; HMS *Good Hope* and HMS *Monmouth*. Both of the British ships were outclassed in both gunnery and seamanship.

In December 1914 von Spee was lured to the Falkland Islands where a Royal Navy task force destroyed his squadron. Of the known German force of eight ships, two escaped: the auxiliary *Seydlitz* and the light cruiser *Dresden*, which roamed at large for a further three months before her captain was cornered by a British squadron off the Juan Fernández Islands on 14 March 1915 and her captain scuttled her by detonating the main ammunition magazine.

Co88 SMS *Gneisenau*. Her gun crews were managing to fire six shells every twenty seconds.

Co90 SMS *Leipzig*.

Co89 SMS *Nürnberg*.

Co93 HMS *Good Hope* had only two big guns and one was destroyed in the first salvo from the *Scharnhorst*. The *Good Hope* was sunk with all hands.

Co91 Rear Admiral Sir Christopher Cradock. The *Good Hope* was his flag ship and, hopelessly outgunned, he went down with her, sunk by the *Scharnhorst*. The *Monmouth* followed sunk by the *Gneisenau*.

Co94 HMS *Monmouth* was pounded by the *Gneisenau* and could only reply with her 6-inch guns firing at their maximum range. There were no survivors from the 700 crew when the *Monmouth* sank.

Co92 HMS *Glasgow* could only look on as the *Good Hope* and the *Monmouth* were used as target practice for the German gunners. Also outgunned she fled the carnage.

Co92 HMS *Canopus* was out of range and was on its way when the battle commenced.

Co95 HMS *Otranto* was an armed merchant vessel and wisely stayed out of range of the guns of the German cruisers.

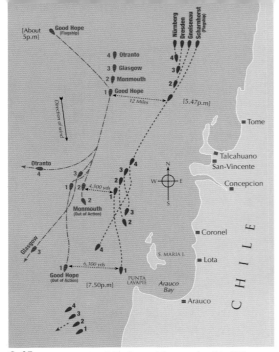

Co95 How the Battle of the Coronel Sea was fought off the coast of Chile.

Co98 The German squadron in the rough seas of the South Atlantic.

After the Battle of the Coronel Sea and the resounding victory over Cradock's inferior ships, German Admiral von Spee and his German East Asia Squadron was about to experience a reversal of fortunes. Following the defeat at Coronel, First Sea Lord Admiral Fisher sent Sturdee to the South Atlantic at the head of a powerful squadron of battle cruisers.

Co100 Admiral von Spee's victorious cruiser squadron anchored at Valparaiso, Chile. The Royal Navy hatched a plot to destroy these ships.

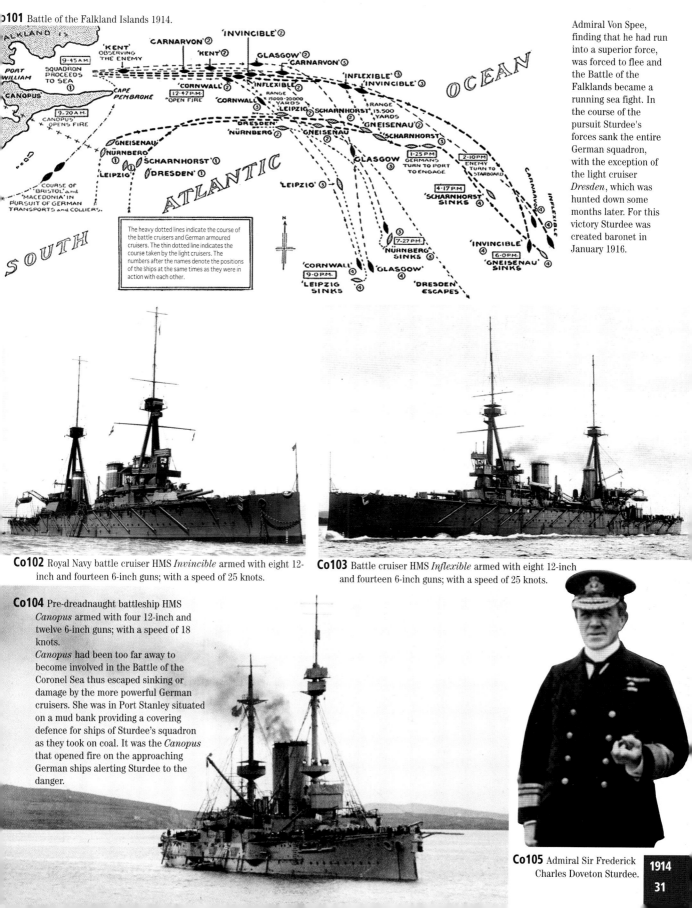

Co101 Battle of the Falkland Islands 1914.

Admiral Von Spee, finding that he had run into a superior force, was forced to flee and the Battle of the Falklands became a running sea fight. In the course of the pursuit Sturdee's forces sank the entire German squadron, with the exception of the light cruiser *Dresden*, which was hunted down some months later. For this victory Sturdee was created baronet in January 1916.

Co102 Royal Navy battle cruiser HMS *Invincible* armed with eight 12-inch and fourteen 6-inch guns; with a speed of 25 knots.

Co103 Battle cruiser HMS *Inflexible* armed with eight 12-inch and fourteen 6-inch guns; with a speed of 25 knots.

Co104 Pre-dreadnaught battleship HMS *Canopus* armed with four 12-inch and twelve 6-inch guns; with a speed of 18 knots.
Canopus had been too far away to become involved in the Battle of the Coronel Sea thus escaped sinking or damage by the more powerful German cruisers. She was in Port Stanley situated on a mud bank providing a covering defence for ships of Sturdee's squadron as they took on coal. It was the *Canopus* that opened fire on the approaching German ships alerting Sturdee to the danger.

Co105 Admiral Sir Frederick Charles Doveton Sturdee.

Co107 German troops at Xmas time carol singing.

Co107 German troops observing Xmas. A painting from the German magazine *Der Krieg 1914/16*.

Co109 Lt Bruce Bainsfather, winter 1914.

Co114 Le Gheer, edge of Ploegsteert Wood, Bruce Bainsfather began his cartooning here, winter 1914.

Co113 Bainsfather does his first cartoon on the wall of a bedroom at Le Gheer, and draws himself doing it.

Co112 Bainsfather captures the Christmas truce of December 1914.

Co106 Lt Bruce Bainsfather.

279 From his new vantage point the French photographer records the arrival of the main force at 12.45.

280 At 5.40 the mayor of Doullens is escorted to the German commandant to discuss the handing over of all forms of transport.

281 Next day the Germans leave Doullens on their way to encircle Paris. The street clock is showing 07.05.

284 Men of the 11th Hussars grabbing a rest during the retreat to the River Marne. Captain the Hon. C. Hulholland assuming a comfortable posture.

285 Wounded being transferred from a French hospital train to a hospital ship for transporting to 'Blighty'.

294 Stretchering wounded aboard a hospital ship at Boulogne.

288 Assisting a walking wounded case to the ship.

290a Walking wounded on their way home from the port of Le Havre.

291a French workers carrying a wounded Highlander on board a ship at Boulogne.

290b Wounded Highlanders on the Folkestone boat.

287 Wounded homeward bound crowd the decks.

287a Wounded at a French dockside waiting for their ship to sail.

294 Stretchering wounded abound.

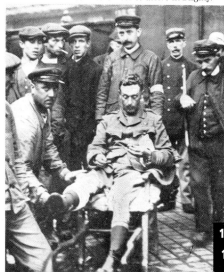

289 A British Tommy awaiting his turn to board falls asleep.

291b Wounded British soldiers arrive on the Folkestone boat and are treated like heroes.

290c The first wounded officer to arrive in Blighty.

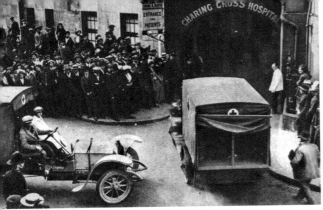

295 Crowds gather outside Charing Cross Hospital to see wounded arrive by ambulance.

293 Wounded on a day out in London are mobbed by admiring crowds.

296 These wounded 'heroes' from the Battle of Mons outside a hospital in England bask in the adoration of young women bearing gifts.

Chapter Six: **Counter Punch – First Battle of the Marne**

297 French infantry during the fighting at the frontiers in August.   **294** French infantry being cheered in the streets of Paris prior to entraining for the Front.

295 French infantry in a Paris street awaiting for orders to move against the German invaders threatening the capital.

300 Motorcycle combination with despatch rider and mascot.

299 French officer addresses his men before leading them off to face the Germans.

296 French artillery with horses decked with flowers.

303 Refreshment on the march.

302 French officer leads his men towards the hordes of German invaders.

301 A French Cuirassier acting as a scout – in shining armour, inappropriate military wear for 20th Century warfare.

304 French cyclists attached to the cavalry. They are carrying folding bicycles called 'bicyclettes' soon to be discarded in the face of modern warfare.

305 The famous French 75mm quick-firing artillery piece with gun crews preparing to fire. It was regarded as the first modern artillery piece. Because its hydro-pneumatic recoil system kept the gun's trail and wheels perfectly still during the firing sequence it did not need to be re-aimed after each shot. This resulted in a high rate of fire – up to 30 rounds per minute with some crews.

306 A machine gun crew preparing to fire.

307 French Reservists.

309 French infantry on the firing line during the Battle of the Marne.

310 Bringing up some medium guns during the Battle of the Marne.

311 German 77mm field gun.

312 Telephone line communication with the gun batteries.

315 German machine gunners.

311 German 77mm field gun ready to lay down covering fire for attacking infantry.

314 German infantry assaulting a French position.

316 French infantry defending their position.

317 Using his dead comrade as cover this French soldier is able to adopt a better firing position. Judging from the height of the camera position this has to be a staged photograph.

318 Germans take cover and begin digging in.

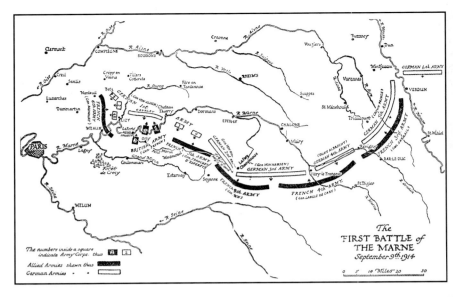

The numbers inside a square indicate Army Corps. thus

Allied Armies shown thus

German Armies

The FIRST BATTLE of THE MARNE
September 9th 1914

0 5 10 Miles 20 30

General Joffre,
Commander-in-Chief

Field Marshal Sir John
French Commander BEF.

General Maunoury.
Sixth Army.

General d'Espéray.
Fifth Army.

General Foch.
Ninth Army.

General Langle de Cary.
Fourth Army.

321 Field Marshal Sir John French in the threatened city of Paris.

General von Kluck.
First Army.

General Heeringen.
Seventh Army.

General von Bülow.
Second Army.

General von Hausen.
Third Army (Aug-Sept).

General Albrecht.
Fourth Army.

General von Einem.
Third Army (From Sept).

Unser Kaiser im Gebet.

Vater im Himmel, Lenker der Sonnen,
Zeuge für mich, der in Demut Dir naht!
Ich nicht habe den Kampf begonnen,
Ich nicht streute die blutige Saat!
Doch von Feinden und Neidern umgeben
Rief ich mein Volk zu eiserner Wehr.
Laß Deinen Geist uns're Waffen umschweben,
Uns sei der Sieg — und Dir sei die Ehr'.

Harry Sheff

320 The Austrian Emperor at prayer. From a postcard issued in Vienna:

Father in Heaven, Ruler of the Universe,
Have pity for him who bows before Thee.
I did not start the strife nor strew the earth with blood.
Surrounded with foes and envy,
I called my people to the defence of arms.
Let Thy mercy surround our lines.
Ours will be the victory and Thine the honour.

319 The Kaiser reviews his troops in northern France in 1914. He is talking to the General commanding the Prussian Guard.

328 Paris defences with its ring of fortifications. The city should have been surrounded according to the German grand plan, but the right wing of the German advance drew in and the plan to take Paris failed. This led to the Battle of the River Marne. See map on page 198.

323 A regiment of Turcos, serving in the French army awaiting the order to march.

336 Military Governor, General Galliéni, reviews French Boy Scouts and members of the Boys' Brigade who have been armed with rifles so as to share in the defence of Paris.

331 A French soldier on guard outside the shell damaged cathedral at Rhiems.

General Joseph Galliéni, tactician behind the French victory in the First Battle of the Marne.

325 French Cuirassiers passing through the streets of Paris on their way to the front receiving gifts of cigarettes from the ladies.

324 A group of French Algerian troops on the outskirts of Paris, strike a pose for the camera.

330 Algerian troops on the approaches to Paris.

322 A French machine gun team having arrived on the outskirts of Paris by taxis and private cars.

326 French infantry massing for an attack.

332 Right: The opening week of September 1914 showing how the Allied forces fought for a distance of seventy miles from La Fère to Paris, where the movement against the German right wing began.

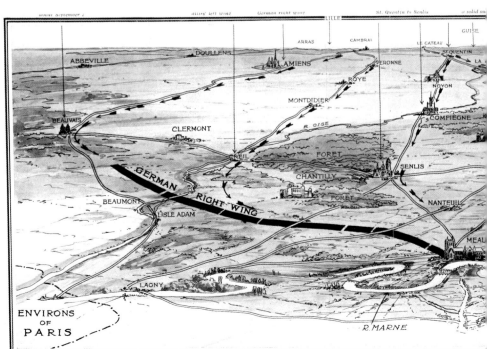

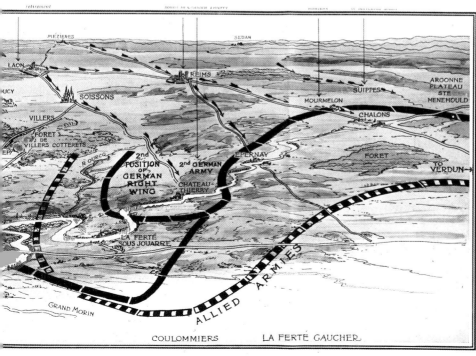

retirement   Sortie la Château Thierry   retirees   in invading army

MÉZIÈRES   SEDAN

LAON

UCY   SOISSONS   REIMS   SUIPPES   ARGONNE PLATEAU STE MENEHOULD

VILLERS   MOURMELON

FORET DE VILLERS COTTERETS   CHALONS

EPY

R. OURCQ   2nd POSITION OF GERMAN RIGHT WING   2nd GERMAN ARMY   EPERNAY   FORET   TO VERDUN

CHATEAU THIERRY

LA FERTÉ SOUS JOUARRE

ALLIED ARMIES

GRAND MORIN

COULOMMIERS   LA FERTÉ GAUCHER

329 French troops marching through the streets on their way to stop the invaders.

335 Mules packed with ammunition and general supplies.

337 French scouts crouching in a meadow littered with gorse bushes.

340 German machine guns in the corn fields of France.

334 Rifles carried at the port by these French infantry who are advancing to a position from which to repel their 'old enemy'.

338 French troops scouting out the German positions.

339 French troops charging the enemy. This is obviously a training exercise, but it captures what took place.

342 French troops charging the enemy.

343 German gun crew laying down fire on the French positions.

341 French soldiers caught by an exploding shell and killed.

344 The body of a German who died of his wounds and was abandoned by his retreating comrades. One of many scattered across the harvested fields in the area of the River Marne, September 1914.

346 Dead of both sides were scattered over a distance of over a hundred miles.

347 German troops withdrawing during the early morning from the French town of Senlis. The closest they got to Paris was just twenty-seven miles away. The French mayor had been held as hostage and when some soldiers were fired upon by towns people he was shot in reprisal and the town was bombarded.

349 A burnt out mansion at Senlis hit in the indiscriminate shelling carried out by the Germans at the time of their withdrawal.

345 Men and horses killed in action were strewn everywhere: some hit by random small arms fire, others by exploding artillery shells and some where units fought it out in bitter hand-to-hand skirmishes.

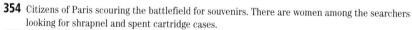

348 French Zouaves collect the remains of those killed in the fighting on the Marne.

354 Citizens of Paris scouring the battlefield for souvenirs. There are women among the searchers looking for shrapnel and spent cartridge cases.

352 Horses presented too large a target on the twentieth-century battlefield.

355 A bicycle expedition to where the fighting took place and these Parisians discover a wrecked car used by the Germans which provides possibilities for finding lost and abandoned valuables.

353 A step too far? Those caught robbing the dead were made to join the local peasantry who were burying the fallen.

356 German dead being buried by the locals. Wages could be found in gold rings, watches and other such personal items.

357 Locals at Meaux burying the dead.

359 French priests find a German still alive.

358 A French soldier's grave with a cross fashioned from mess tin handles. Also the man's cap.

351 Bridges on the approaches to Paris were destroyed to prevent the invader from taking the capitol. Blown-up bridge at St Maxence over the Cise.

361 Road bridge over the Marne at Lagny, blown up by French engineers as the Germans approached.

362 A bridge over the Marne destroyed by the Germans at La Ferté-sous-Jouarre. The Germans were retreating and it was here where the BEF crossed under fire to give chase.

363 Royal Engineers with bridging material in France 1914.

365 Passage over the Marne, D Company, 1st Cameronians crossing a pontoon bridge built by the royal Engineers at La Ferté-sous-Jouarre, 10 September 1914.

A memorial commemorates the event and the inscription reads: *At this point was built under fire by the Royal Engineers of the 4th Division a floating bridge for the passage of the left wing of the British Expeditionary Force after the Battle of the Marne.* Portions of the division had already crossed by boat at the weir near Luzancy and below the destroyed bridge.

360 Iron bridge over the Marne at Lagny, blown up by the French.

364 Discarded German equipment abandoned during their retreat from the Marne. French cavalry pose wearing captured German Picklehaube helmets. Three German prisoners look on unamused.

368 French cavalry crossing the Marne by a pontoon bridge.

367 Abandoned German artillery limber wagons.

370 A wrecked German ammunition wagon at Melle.

369 Captured German guns bound for England.

350 Abandoned loot: a piano rests in the middle of a field; too heavy for the Germans to carry with them.

373 British cavalry escorting the British General Staff on the move in northern France.

371 A heavily damaged German 77 mm field gun in a firing position with its limber.

372 Bengal Lancers following up the German retreat. They are organized into four squadrons composed variously of Punjab Mussulmans, Sikhs, Jats, Dogras, Pathans, Mahrattas and Rajputs. Described as the pick of the fighting races of the East.

374 A detachment of the Scotts Greys (2nd Dragoons); useful in a war of movement, which the Great War was in the opening months.

375 French walking wounded.

376 A party of Sikhs with their pack horses. They are identified as Sikhs by a metal circular badge worn on the turban.

377 French cavalry riding past the 1st Cameronians in bivouac, where, with the rest of 19 Brigade, the Cameronian Highlanders lay hidden all day and then at night they took to the roads and were free from observation by German spotter aircraft.

378 German prisoners escorted by French cavalry being marched to prisoner of war camps near Paris.

379 An Algerian cavalryman fighting for France.

Chapter Seven: First Battle of the Aisne – First Battle of Ypres

380 British artillery position on the Aisne.

381 Tommy arrives by civilian transport and receives a warm welcome in this French town.

384 British occupying the town of Braisne where heavy fighting took place in this street. The Germans fired from the houses where they had waited to ambush the pursuing Allies.

387 A German regiment on the march. The invaders were falling back to the River Aisne.

388 British artillery and French cavalry share the same road as they pursue the withdrawing enemy.

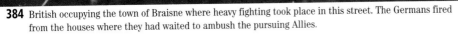

385 French on the heels of the Hun pass by a vineyard in northern France.

386 Full marching order.

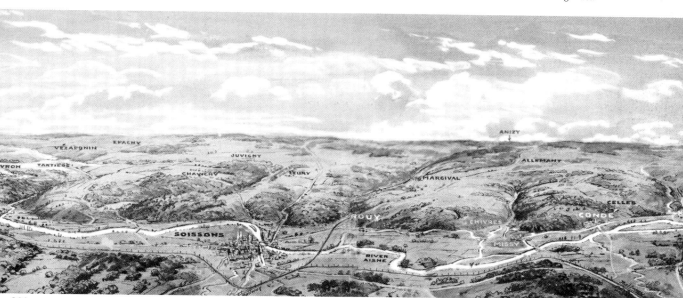

382 A depiction of the Aisne river valley along which the opposing forces would face each other to fight the Battle of the Aisne.

389 German cavalry on a wet early autumn day.

390 British despatch riders try to seek directions.

392 French officers of various units seeking to locate the enemies' positions.

395 A road leading to the Allies' positions during the fighting on the Aisne showing halted French transport.

396 French soldiers in a forest bivouac in the fighting area.

393 The French town of Soissons, situated by the River Aisne, was the scene of heavy fighting. It was here that British troops crossed the river.

394 Dead civilians near the bridge at Soissons. The original caption hopes to persuade the reader that they are, in fact, dead Germans.

397 British infantry dug in to slit trenches and dug-outs on the Aisne.

399 German infantry digging a shallow line of trenches.

403 Keeping a close eye on the Allied lines.

400 Parallel with and on both sides of the River Aisne the opposing armies dug in and an intense period of shelling began. The German had their heavy artillery in quarries behind the ridge and, supported by field guns, they poured a rain of shells onto the British and French positions.

401 Machine gun position of the 1st Cameronians in the front line at St Marguerite, 24 September 1914, during the fighting either side of the Aisne river.

398 The firing line.

404 German shells dropping into the streets of Soissons smashed houses and caught these horses.

405 Shells bursting over Soissons.

412 British 6-inch howitzer battery moving up on the Aisne.

409 Royal Artillery in action on the Aisne.

406 A lull in the fighting at Soissons. A mixture of men involved: an African Chasseur; two Turcos; three British infantrymen; a French civilian and two British officers dressed in civilian clothes.

410 A 18-pounder gun crew during the Battle of the Aisne.

414 German infantry manning shallow trenches.

412 British heavy artillery moving up on the Aisne.

409 A German officer and six men taking cover behind a pile of wood have been caught and killed by a single shell from a French 75 mm field gun.

415 German heavy artillery bombarding the Allied positions on the Aisne.

407 An ambulance is seriously damaged by a near miss in the streets of Soissons.

408 A British stretcher bearer tending the wounds of a German soldier.

416 French soldiers killed by a shell.

417 Algerian Tirailleurs, or Turcos, killed while charging a German position.

418 French and German fallen side by side. The body in the foreground is a German and the ones behind are French.

419 The French have dug a mass grave to bury around 300 dead Germans. They appear to be using quick lime spread over the corpses and covering over with earth as the trench is being filled.

421 Individual markers placed over the graves of buried German soldiers.

420 British shelters connected to the trench system on the Aisne. The beginnings of what would later become more permanent dwellings for the duration of the war over the next four years.

422 German officers' dugout: shelters would become ever more elaborate once the war of movement had come to an end by December 1914.

425 German 210 mm heavy howitzer, which could lob a shell over four miles.

428 Germans hauling a 21 cm heavy howitzer into position.

426 A shell exploded in this street in Soissons a few minutes before the photograph was taken. Civilians are tending the wounded horse.

427 Inhabitants of Rheims sleeping in one of the wine vaults during a German bombardment.

424 German heavy howitzer in search of a target.

437 The French cathedral at Rheims proved to be a useful aiming point for the Germans.

429 A French soldier stands guard at the door of the heavily damaged Rheims cathedral.

430 Indian and English soldiers buying drinks before setting off on a series of attempts to outflank the German line along the Aisne. The Tommy with the six years Good Conduct Stripes is also wearing a Gun-layer's badge above them.

435 Indian cavalry.

431 Northward from the Aisne: British cavalry in the Doullens district in the drive towards Flanders.

433 Men of the 59th Field Company Royal Engineers ready to move out.

432 Motorcycle with sidecar and a Vickers machine gun behind armour plate.

445 German shelters behind the lines on the Aisne.

450 German Uhlans leaving a French town.

440 The Germans also were seeking an open flank to turn. German scouts watering their horses in a French village.

449 German Uhlans following up the scouts.

444 German shelters behind the lines on the Aisne.

446 German field kitchen in operation.

443 The Germans hold a kit inspection.

451 A marching German column halted in the streets of a French town.

447 German column marching north.

438 A British field gun battery on the move across open ground during the flanking movement.

441 French cavalry on the roads heading north.

445 German shelters behind the lines on the Aisne.

448 A French sniper. Note the bayonet, for his Lebel rifle, nicknamed 'Rosalie'.

436 A British infantry battalion on the march through French countryside.

452 British Lancers exchanging banter with their Allies.

455 A poster to help identify German aeroplanes.

453 These French sharpshooters have spotted an aircraft – friend or foe? Aircraft recognition was, like aviation, in its infancy.

459 The first Royal Flying Corps aircraft to fly to France, piloted by Major Harvey-Kelly. The machine is a B.E.2C of No.2 Squadron.

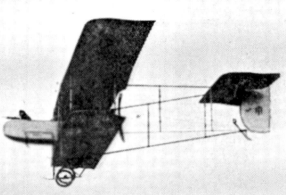

454 A Taube scout plane being chased off by a French biplane.
457 German aircraft types employed in scouting out the moving armies.

456 An early French attempt to mount a machine gun on an aircraft.

461 French turn their machine gun against aircraft.   **460** Parisians watching a Taube scout plane circling the city.

463 How the first bombs were dropped. Crewman of Royal Naval Flying Corps takes aim.

462 German air scouts receiving instruction via telephone link to headquarters.

465 British aviators receive instructions before taking off to locate the latest German positions as the opposing armies race to outflank each other.

464 A Pfalz scout aeroplane.

466 British infantry marching north towards Ypres.

468 A British advance unit halts outside a French village.

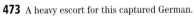

469 Searching through the empty streets.

473 A heavy escort for this captured German.

472 A British heavy artillery column.

471 A German sniper lurking behind a haystack.

470 A German sniper has been located and shot dead.

474 Marketplace of Thielt, north east of Ypres, Belgium. The 2nd Battalion Scots Guards filling the square, 12 October 1914.

475 The 11th Hussars make a halt in the town of Bonnières.

476 German mounted patrol seeking to contact the enemy.

543 2nd Battalion Scots Guards digging trenches near Ghent 9 October.

477 Reconnaissance force of the 2nd Scots Guards at Gheluvelt.

480 Taking up firing positions across a road near Ypres, these men of the 2nd Royal Scots Fusiliers prepare to stop the German advance.

480 2nd Royal Scots Fusiliers digging a trench at Terhand, near Gheluvelt.

482 British cavalry arrives in the square at Ypres 13 October 1914. A defensive salient would form around this Belgian town and it would be fought over for the next four years. The buildings shown here would be reduced to piles of rubble.

484 British soldiers in front of the Claustrum St Martini, in the town of Ypres. A German shell has destroyed the building alongside. Within days the town would begin to be pounded to destruction.

485 Another building wrecked in the same bombardment as the above. An eyewitness account dated 16 November 1914 reads: *As each successive attempt to take Ypres by assault fails, the bombardment of the unhappy town is renewed with increasing fury.*

488 Interior of the Cloth Hall, Ypres during the early bombardment. The roof is off and British soldiers have tethered their horses to the medieval pillars where once merchants of Ypres conducted their business.

487 The Cloth Hall, Ypres during the early bombardment. The tower proved to be an ideal aiming point for the German artillery.

493 German howitzer pounding the Allied postions in Belgium.

489 German artillery.

490 German 77 mm gun crew.

491 The western end of the Cloth Hall at Ypres after the initial bombardment.

492 Claustrum St Martini at Ypres with the building on the right side of the colonade wrecked by German artillery fire.

495 The church of St. Martin at Ypres.

494 Ypres in the process of being reduced to rubble.

496 British troops leaving a French town and returning to their units after recovering from illnesses, accidents or slight wounds.

498 Very welcome letters from home being distributed to men of the 19th Infantry Brigade at a roadside farmhouse during the First Battle of Ypres, October 1914.

499 Cyclists of a signals section arrive in a Belgian village in the Ypres Salient.

497 Men of the 2nd Scots Guards arriving at billets in Zillebeke after being relieved by French troops in the Ypres Salient.

500 British infantry preparing a meal.

501 British transport wagons on the Menin Road during the First Battle of Ypres.

502 The Northumberland Hussars, a Yeomanry regiment, resting in Sanctuary Wood.

504 Tree trunks blocking this road leading to Ypres.

503 Infantry of the 7th Division seek to identify where they are, and where they are going.

505 A wounded cavalryman, after being patched up is escorted to a dressing station.

506 Britsh infantry manning some defence positions in the Ypres Salient.

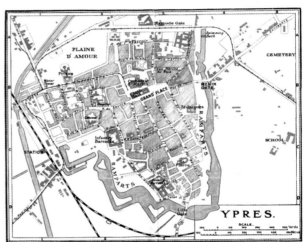

Street map of Ypres showing the old defence system.

509 British soldiers using the old ramparts at Ypres as billets.

513 British soldiers await the attacking Germans.

507 German artillery passing infantry in the Ypres sector.

508 A German Uhlan patrol.

510 German Uhlans crossing a river in Belgium.

512 British soldiers await the attacking Germans, each man intent on employing his fifteen aimed shots per minute.

514 German infantry in mid bayonet charge.

517 A field of German dead in the aftermath of their bayonet charge.

522 Lieutenant General Gough, commanding 2nd British Cavalry Division discusses the situation with two members of his staff.

523 Lieutenant General Gough, with two of his staff officers.

515 Machine gun section guarding a road.

516 Awaiting the enemy.

518 Germans observing the effects of the fighting.

521 German machine gun crew operating a Maxim 08.

524 Men of the 2nd Battalion Scots Guards dug in at Ypres, October 1914.

525 Men of the 2nd Battalion Scots Guards behind the lines at Ypres, October 1914.

526 Men of the Ox and Bucks Light Infantry behind the lines at Ypres.

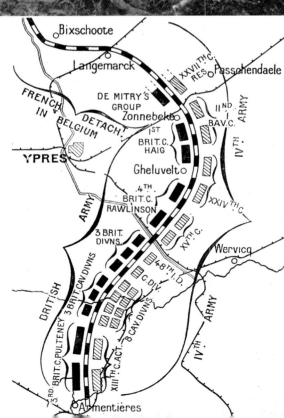

529 Duke of Connaught inspects men of the 14th (County of London) Battalion, The London Regiment (London Scottish).

530 Pipers of the 14th (County of London) Battalion, The London Regiment (London Scottish) passing Buckingham Palace, September 1914 .

542 Pipers of the London Scottish leading the battalion down Whitehall, September 1914.

529 Medicals being carried out on new recruits.

532 London Scottish marching to Watford Station 15 September 1914.

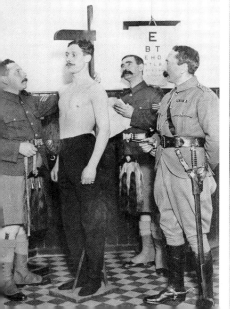

532 London Scottish arriving at Watford Station, 15 September 1914, and entraining for Southampton.

The 14th (County of London) Battalion, The London Regiment (London Scottish) was the first Territorial Army infantry battalion to be sent to France. They sailed from Southampton on the SS *Winifredian*.

533 Men of the London Scottish grab a bite to eat on a French railway station.

534 London Scottish in their 'skirts' which arouse curiosity. Upon arriving in France the battalion was dispersed and was employed on line-of-communication duties throughout northern France. The men here, working on overhead telegraph wires, have decided to suspend their activities for some reason.

545 London Scottish at their morning ablutions in a French town.

546 A group of London Scottish in France.

547 Kitted out in full marching order.

550 London buses used to transport troops to the front. These are men of the 2nd Battalion, the Warwickshire Regiment.

548 A painting depicting the London Scottish arriving at the town of Ypres by London double-decker buses.

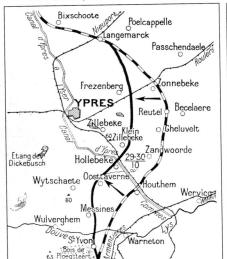

551 October 29-30: German thrust to take Ypres

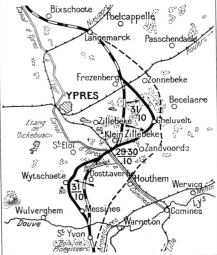

552 October 31: The Germans made progress to the south of Ypres but were driven back towards Gheluvelt.

553 November 1: The Germans captured the Messines-Wytschaete ridge. The British fell back on Wulverghem.

556 German Uhlan, dismounted and engaging the enemy with rifle fire.

535 Sergeants of the London Scottish rest during their march towards Wytschaete.

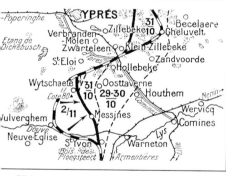

554 November 2: The French counter-attacked and retook the Messines-Wytschaete ridge. The Germans launched a mass attack against Gheluvelt.

555 November 11: The Germans finally ceased in their attempts to capture Ypres until the following year – April 1915.

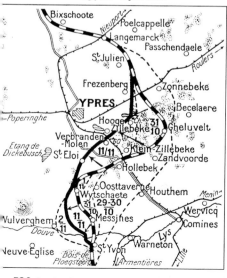

536 London Scottish resting on the Hooge Road, 30 October.

557 A British artist's interpretation of the involvement of the London Scottish in the Battle of Messines. He even depicted the jamming of British rifles experienced during the fighting.

556 German infantry massing for an assault on the Allied positions.

538 The roll call near Wolvergham after the Battle of Messines. Only 150 officers and men answered. In the days that followed stragglers turned up and finally it was accounted that 394 officers and men had been killed or were missing.

540 The 1st Guards Brigade after the Battle of Ypres. In the brigade with the London Scottish were the 1st Battalion Black Watch, 1st Battalion Scots Guards, 1st Coldstream Guards and the 1st Cameron Highlanders.

541 An interpretation by a German artist, G. Koch, of the fighting during the Battle of Messines. Compare with the British artist's painting on the same spot on opposite page.

539 After the Battle of Messines. With minimal training at the front; without maps; with mal-functioning rifles and without the support of their machine guns the Territorial battalion had met a superior number of the enemy and stopped its advance on Ypres.

558 A few of the London Scottish, survivors of the fighting, marching off to billets near Bailleul, via La Clytte.

560 Indian troops arrived in France in October and were fully committed in December.

562 French Algerian cavalry escorting German prisoners.

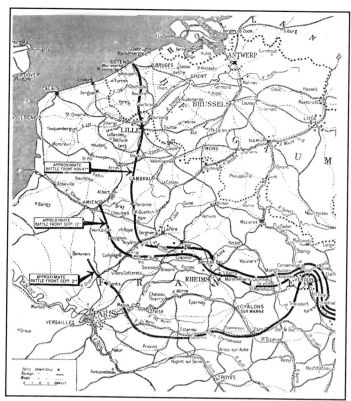

559 Approximate battle positions from September to November 1914.

560/561 Indian troops, part of the BEF, with Maxim machine guns. Some elements fought in the Battle of Ypres, 1914.

563 German infantry among the sand dunes at the North Sea coast in Belgium.

566 Germans among the sand dunes tending a comrade's grave.

567 Belgians face the Germans across the flooded countryside.

567 Germans manning Pom Pom gun positions

565 *Küstenartillerie in Tätigkeit* Coastal artillery in action.

568/569 The Belgian town of Pervyse, between Nieuport and Dixmude. The pictures were taken just after it was recaptured from the Germans.

478 German infantrymen strike a pose for the camera.

Chapter Eight: Exchanging Broadsides – Fighting at Sea

570 The 2 Squadron of the German High Seas Fleet sails out to the North Sea.

571 A Royal Navy battleship taking torpedoes on board.

573 On 5 August 1914 HMS *Amphion* was acting as a scout cruiser based at Harwich when her crew were alerted to a German minelayer, the *Königin Luise*, working in the North Sea. The *Amphion* attacked and sank the *Königin Luise* but next day sailed over one of the German mines.

574 The German minelayer *Königin Luise*. Her sinking, along with the *Amphion*, was the first naval action of the war.

577 A last salute for the eight men, British and German, buried together with full military honours.

572 HMS *Amphion* among a screen of Destroyers. The *Amphion* sailed into the minefield laid by the *Königin Luise* and was sunk. One officer, 148 men and 18 German prisoners from the *Königin Luise* lost their lives. There were 139 survivors.

575 A German mine being lowered into a U-boat.

576 German and British sailors, four German and four British from the *Königin Luise* and *Amphion* buried together. Two Salvation Army officers were in attendance.

578 Captain Cecil Henry Fox, HMS *Amphion*.

579 A German war artist depicts the moment HMS *Amphion* strikes the mine laid by the *Königin Luise*

580 British trawlers equipped as minesweepers.

A member of the crew of HMS *Birmingham*, Able Seaman Pearson, described the action to his father in a letter:

When the firing started the periscope was blown away, then she came to the top. All our guns were trained on her and before she was hit the second time she switched on a small light and an officer came up into the conning tower. Just as he poked his head up a shell hit the tower and blew it and him to atoms. Then she sank.
It is the first action I've been in, but I hope it isn't the last. I am dying to get at the Germans and blow them to atoms, for it makes my blood boil to read about the way they are serving brave men. I am itching to have a go at them.

Birmingham Pals *by Terry Carter*

583 The light cruiser HMS *Birmingham* sank the first German U-boat of the war on Sunday 9 August. The Royal Navy 1st Light Cruiser Squadron was patroling off the German coast when it was attacked by a German submarine flotilla. The U-boats were submerged with just their periscopes above water. As the nearest submarine, *U-15*, came within range the *Birmingham* fired and hit the periscope. The second shot wrecked the conning tower and the *U-15* sank with all hands.

581 German mine.

582 A German mine exploded under the bow of this trawler. Between 27 August and 3 September four trawlers were lost after hitting mines in the North Sea.

584 The U-15 sunk by the cruiser HMS *Birmingham* four days after the declaration of war. While stranded on the surface repairing her engines she was spotted through a thick fog. The *Birmingham* opened fire but missed. As U-15 attempted to dive she was rammed and cut in half, killing all 23 members of its crew. This is a different version of the action to the one given by the able seaman opposite.

585 British war artist, Norman Wilkinson, depicted the sinking of the U-15 in the manner described by the eye-witness.

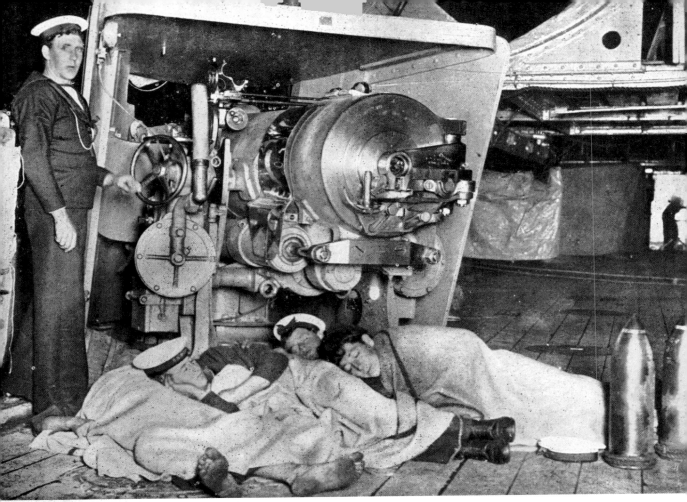

586 Sleeping by the guns: nighttime on board a British cruiser.

590 Stokers in the engine room of a British cruiser.

591 Loading a torpedo into the hold of a British cruiser.

587a Former German liner *Kaiser Wilhelm Der Grosse* had been turned into an armed raider. She was sunk off West Africa by HMS *Highflyer* in August 1914.

588 *Korvettenkapitan* Paul Reymann captain of the *Kaiser Wilhelm Der Grosse*.

589 HMS *Highflyer,* former Public School boys' training ship, sank the armed commerce raider *Kaiser Wilhelm Der Grosse* off the mouth of the River Oro, West Africa.

592 Preparing a mine aboard a Royal Navy minelayer.

602 Captain H.T. Buller, HMS *Highflyer.*

594 Heligoland is located 29 miles off the German coastline and consists of two islands. It guarded the approaches to the German naval bases.

596 Kaiser Wilhelm II, in the uniform of the German Navy.

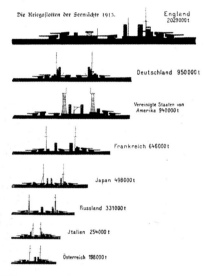

Die Kriegsflotten der Seemächte 1913.

England 2029000 t

Deutschland 950000 t

Vereinigte Staaten von Amerika 940000 t

Frankreich 646000 t

Japan 498000 t

Russland 331000 t

Jtalien 254000 t

Österreich 198000 t

595 A comparison of the tonnage of fighting ships of the world's navies published in the German magazine *Der Krieg 1914 in Wort und Bild*.

598 The Kaiser on a tour of inspection.

600 The German High Seas Fleet anchored in Kiel harbour at the Baltic end of the Kaiser Wilhelm Canal.

597 German Naval Base at Wilhelmshaven.

599 The Kaiser with some of his sailors at Wilhelmshaven.

603 Heligoland where the first naval battle of the war was fought on 28 August 1914 in a sea known as the Heligoland Bight. The island had been fortified by the Germans and it served as a base for patrol craft.

606 Moorings for battleships at Wilhelmshaven.

607 *Grossadmiral* von Tirpitz, Secretary of State for the German Imperial Navy.

605 *Grossadmiral* Prince Heinrich von Preussen, brother of the Kaiser. He guarded the German coast against attacks by the Russian fleet.

608 German sailors swabbing the deck on a Nassau class dreadnaught.

601 German High Seas Fleet venturing out of the harbours at Wilhelmshaven.

609 German sailors enjoying the sun aboard the SMS *Elsass* of the last pre dreadnaught Braunschweig class battleships in the German Imperial Navy. Her keel was laid down in 1901.

610 Georg Alexander von Müller, Chief of the German Imperial Naval Cabinet

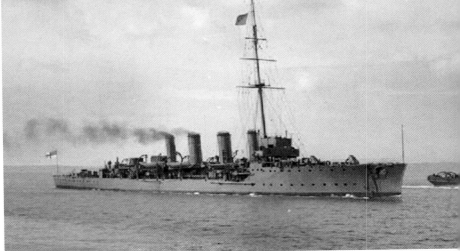

593 Admiral Jellicoe, Royal Navy Commander-in-Chief.

612 HMS *Fearless* the cruiser which helped decoy elements of the German fleet into venturing out to attack a light force of British Royal Navy vessels sailing near Heligoland.

614 One of the Royal Navy destroyers which took part in the action off Heligoland, HMS *Liberty*.

617 Lieutenant-Commander Nigel Bartellot killed aboard HMS *Liberty* during the action at Heligoland Bight. One of two naval officers to die.

611 German light Cruiser *Mainz*, with two funnels blown away, seen here sinking following action with the Royal Navy First Battle-Cruiser Squadron.

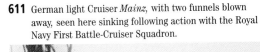

618 German Light Cruiser SMS *Ariadne* sunk at the Battle of Heligoland Bight with loss of 200 lives.

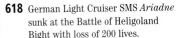

613 Cruiser HMS *Arethusa* led a Royal Navy destroyer flotila to attack the German cruisers which had been drawn into a fight.

615 German light Cruiser *Mainz* sunk by the Royal Navy First Light Cruiser Squadron

619 German minesweeper *D8* showing damage from one of five shells which struck her. The metal is heavily bloodstained.

620 HMS *Lion* was in the Heligoland Bight action.

621 HMS *Queen Mary* was in the Heligoland Bight action.

622 HMS *Princess Royal* was in the Heligoland Bight action.

622 HMS *New Zealand* was in the Heligoland Bight action.

624 HMS *Invincible* was in the Heligoland Bight action.

623 HMS *Lion, Princess Royal* and *Queen Mary* three Royal Navy battle cruisers seen steaming together.

616 Vice-Admiral Sir David Beatty, commander of the First Battle-Cruiser Squadron.

626 SMS *Köln* sunk by HMS *Lion*. One of three German cruisers sunk in the action off Heligoland.

Commodore Reginald Tyrwhitt and Commodore Roger Keyes devised the plan to ambush destroyers engaged in their regular patrols in the North Sea. A fleet of thirty-one destroyers, two cruisers under Tyrwhitt and submarines commanded by Keyes was dispatched. They were supported with back-up by an additional six light cruisers commanded by Commodore William Goodenough and five battlecruisers commanded by Vice Admiral David Beatty.

Three German light cruisers and one destroyer were sunk. Three more light cruisers were damaged, 712 sailors killed, 530 injured and 336 taken prisoner. The British suffered one light cruiser and three destroyers damaged, 35 killed and 40 wounded.

The battle was regarded as a great victory in Britain, where the returning ships were met by cheering crowds. In the eyes of the British public, Vice Admiral Beatty was regarded as a hero, although he had taken little part in the action or planning. However, the raid might have led to disaster had the additional forces under Beatty not been sent by Admiral John Jellicoe at the last minute.

THE BATTLE OF THE HELIGOLAND BIGHT.
THE FIRST NAVAL ENGAGEMENT OF THE WAR

ABRAHAMS & SONS,
DEVONPORT.

632 SMS *Mainz* sinking during the Battle of Heligoland Bight. A Royal Navy destroyer races to pick up survivors.

629 Commodore Reginald Tyrwhitt, in command of the destroyer flotillas of the First Fleet. He, along with Commodore Roger Keyes, planned the attack on the German fleet destroyers patroling in the vicinity of the German sea base at Heligoland. The resulting victory had a serious inhibiting effect on operations of the Kaiser's fleet.

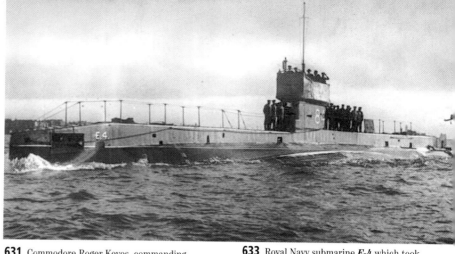

631 Commodore Roger Keyes, commanding the submarine flotilla.

633 Royal Navy submarine *E-4* which took part in the Heligoland action.

634 Rear Admiral Sir Gordon Moore.

635 Commodore William Edmund Goodenough.

636 Rear Admiral H. A. Christian.

638/637 The victorious Royal Navy patroling the North Sea in 1914.

639 Two German battleships the SMS *Kaiser* and the *Kaiserin* at their berths in the Kiel Canal. The effect of the Royal Naval victory at Heligoland Bight upon the German government, in particular the Kaiser, was to restrict the freedom of action of the German fleet, instructing it to remain in port and avoid any contact with superior forces.

640 German U-boats with light cruisers in the distance. Reliance on submarines and mine-layers would gain in importance as the method of waging the war at sea for the German navy.

641 Crowds on the quayside at Heligoland greet a German U-boat returning from sorté against merchant vessels and Royal Naval ships.

642 A German trawler equipped for laying mines is being prepared for a mission.

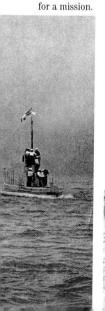

643 Minesweeper HMS *Speedy* was leading a party of minesweepers off the Humber when she went to pick up survivors from another vessel which had struck a mine and ran onto one herself. She sank with the loss of one life.

644 *Kapitänleutnant* Otto Hersing, commander of *U-21*.

647 HMS *Pathfinder* was acting as flotilla leader for the 8th Destroyer Flotilla and was returning to the Royal Naval Base at Rosyth in Scotland to take on coal. Otto Hersing attacked with one torpedo which struck the forward magazine causing a massive explosion which totally destroyed the forepart of the ship. She sank within minutes and over 250 sailors lost their lives. There were just twelve survivors.

645 German submarine of the type commanded by Hersing and which sank HMS *Pathfinder*.

646 German U-boat with a torpedo track. Crew of the *Pathfinder* saw it coming but could not change course in time.

648/649 Views of the Royal Naval Base at Rosyth in Scotland (postcard and aerial photograph).

650 SMS *Königsberg* was a German commerce raider operating in the Indian Ocean and attacking merchant ships in the Red Sea area.

653 HMS *E8* sister vessel to Commander Horton's *E9*.

654 Lieutenant-Commander Max K. Horton in submarine *E9* sank a German light cruiser 13 September. The following month he attacked and sank the German torpedo-boat *S126* off the mouth of the Ems River.

651 Max Looff captain of SMS *Königsberg*.

647 HMS *Pegasus* was undergoing repairs in the harbour at Zanzibar when the German commerce raider *Königsberg* sailed up and opened fire. With her guns out of action she was a floating wreck and sank later that day, 20 September. Thirty-eight British sailors were killed.

656 SMS *Hela* sunk by the *E9* six miles south of Heligoland on 13 September.

655 German torpedo-boat *S126* cutting through the seas at full steam.

657 *E9* moored between *E4* and *E5*.

Unterseeboot 9 (26 Mann Besatzung)
welches bei seinem heldenmütigen Angriff am 22. Sept. 1914
drei englische Panzerkreuzer vernichtete.

Kapitänleutnant Weddigen (Otto), Kommandant,
Oberleutnant zur See Spieß,
Marineingenieur Schoen,
Obersteuermann Traebert,
Obermaschinist Heinemann,
Bootsmannsmaate: Schöppe, Heer,
Matrosen: Geist, Rosenaus, Schenker, Schulz,
Obermaschinistenmaate: Merlow, Stellmacher, Hinrichs,
Maschinistenmaate: Maerz, Reichardt,
Obermaschinistenanwärter: Wollenberg, v. Koslowski,
Oberheizer: Rheinbütter, Schöschke,
Heizer: Karbe, Scholer, Lied, Köster, Vollstedt,
Funkenheizer: Sievers.

663 Postcard commemorating the event of the sinking of three Royal Navy light cruisers in the same action 22 September.

662 Captain of the *U9*, *Kapitänleutnant* Otto Weddigen, photographed with his wife.

On 22 September, U-9 located a squadron of three obsolescent British Cressy-class armoured cruisers the *Aboukir*, *Hogue* and *Cressy*, (nicknamed the "Live Bait Squadron") which had been assigned to cover approaches to the eastern end of the English Channel. She fired six torpedoes, reloading while submerged, and sank all three British ships in less than an hour. 1,459 sailors died. It was one of the most notable submarine actions of all time. Those in the Admiralty who had viewed submarines as little more than curiosities changed their minds after this Royal Navy disaster.

Rear Admiral Henry Campbell and Rear Admiral Arthur Christian were relieved of their commands by a court of enquiry after being found guilty of serious errors of judgement.

658 HMS *Aboukir*.

659 HMS *Hogue*.
660 HMS *Cressy*.

661 The German submarine U9 following her sinking of three Royal Navy cruisers.

664 HMS *Hawke* was the victim of the German submarine *U9*, *Kapitänleutnant* Otto Weddigen. She was hit by a single torpedo, whereupon she turned over and sank off the north coast of Scotland. Over 500 sailors lost their lives.

665 HMS *Audacious* sinking after hitting a mine off the Irish coast. News was suppressed in the United Kingdom for reasons of morale, it being a superdreadnaught.

666 Postcard extolling the mightiness of the superdreadnaught HMS *Audacious*.

H.M.S. AUDACIOUS. Battleship, 23,600 tons.
Cost £1,985,000. Length, 555 feet; Beam, 89 feet; Draught, 27½ feet; Speed, 21¼ knots. Armed with Ten 13.5; Sixteen 4 in.; Four Small Quick Firing Guns, and Three Torpedo Tubes.

667 Victorious U*9* returning to base after sinking three British cruisers.

670 HMS *Hermes* seaplane carrier, sunk by U*27*, 31 October.

672 HMS *Hermes* sinking in the Dover Straits with the loss of 44 hands.

669 SMS *Scharnhorst*, von Spee's flag ship.

668 Vice Admiral Maximilian Reichsgraf von Spee commanded the German East Asia Squadron.

671 Vice Admiral von Spee's ships leaving Valparaiso, Chile, to engage the British South American Squadron which had been reported off Coronel. The British squadron consisted of three cruisers and was outgunned by Spee's five cruisers.

673 Rear Admiral Christopher Craddock, British South American Squadron.

674 HMS *Good Hope* Rear Admiral Craddock's flagship. She was leading the squadron to attack von Spee's squadron and was sunk by the SMS *Scharnhorst*, von Spee's flag ship. There were no survivors

675 Some of the crew of HMS *Monmouth* resting during coaling. All would lose their lives in the Coronel Sea action, 1 November.

Battle of the Coronel Sea. On 22 October, 1914, Craddock's South American Squadron sailed from the Falkland Islands, around the Cape of Good Hope, to try and locate the German squadron reported to be off the west coast of South America. Craddock's squadron consisted of two armoured cruisers and one light cruiser; also a lightly-armoured merchant vessel. He was seeking out two German armoured cruisers and three light cruisers manned by seasoned sailors expert in gunnery. The British admiral's ships were hopelessly outgunned and yet he sailed to meet Spee's squadron head on. With the setting sun silhouetting the British ships von Spee opened fire. The German shooting was very accurate and the *Scharnhorst* gunners straddled the *Good Hope* then, with the target sighted up, proceeded to sink her. HMS *Monmouth* likewise was targetted by the *Gneisenau* and then the *Scharnhorst* joined in. Attempts by the captain of HMS *Monmouth*, Captain Frank Brandt, to escape failed and the German cruiser *Nürnberg* came across her burning and listing heavily. She did not return fire, and because she was still flying her battle ensign the captain of the *Nürnberg* carried on firing at point blank range until the *Monmouth* turned over and sank. There were no survivors.

679 HMS *Glasgow* escaped with moderate damage considering an estimated 600 shells were fired at her.

674 HMS *Monmouth*. She was no match for the German ships with her 6-inch guns and was finished off by SMS *Nürnberg* during the final stages of the fight.

677 German cruiser SMS *Gneisenau* with her 8-inch guns took part in the sinking of the *Monmouth*.

678 German light cruiser SMS *Nürnberg* finished off the crippled *Monmouth*.

682 The *Emden* at the German base at Tsingtao in July 1914.

692 *Korvettenkapitän* Karl Friedrich Max von Müller.

691 SMS *Emden* German light cruiser.

707 *Leutnant zur See*
Hellmuth von Mücke.

At one time up to sixty Allied warships were combing the Indian Ocean in the search for the *Emden*. Beginning in September, she had begun to prey upon the hundreds of unescorted British and Allied merchant ships. She captured seventeen ships and sank them by fire from her 10.5 cm (4.1 inch) guns or by placed explosive charges. Captain Müller was always gentlemanly to the captains and passengers of the ships he captured making sure that every sailor and passenger was well treated.

In view of the commerce raider's amazing success the British Admiralty stopped all British shipping on the Colombo-Singapore route. This caused panic among the British and Allied shipping offices in the Indian Ocean. Shipping companies could not afford to leave harbour. It was a source of embarrassment to the British that a single German cruiser could effectively shut down the entire Indian Ocean.

On 9 November 1914 *Emden* reached Direction Island and Müller sent a fifty-strong landing party ashore to destroy the station's radio tower and equipment. However, it had been noted that the cruiser had three funnels and a suspicious operator of the Eastern Telegraph Company radioed that an unidentified warship was in the area. In under three hours the Australian light cruiser, HMAS *Sydney*, arrived after sailing at top speed. When lookouts spotted the *Sydney* approaching, Captain von Müller had no choice but to raise anchor, leave his landing party on Direction Island, and engage the Australian cruiser.

Sydney was larger and faster than *Emden* and outranged her, but still the fight went on for nearly an hour and a half. Early on, *Emden* managed to knock out a gun on *Sydney* and destroy the rangefinder. But *Emden* hit over 100 times and suffered serious damage. Her firing dwindled and Captain von Müller beached *Emden* on North Keeling Island to avoid sinking.

German losses were 131 dead and 65 wounded. Captain von Müller and the rest of his crew were made prisoners of war. The officers were, however, allowed to retain their swords as a mark of honour.

The landing party under Lieutenant von Mücke had hoisted the Imperial German flag, declaring the island a German possession. He then commandeered a sailing vessel, a three-masted schooner *Ayesha* and departed for Padang, Sumatra, and safety.

Die Taten der Emden

Hafen von Pulo-Pinang

30. Oktober 1914
Die Emden vernichtete den russischen Kreuzer
„Szhemtschug" und einen französischen Torpedojäger

696 A German postcard commemorating the actions of SMS *Emden* in the Indian Ocean.

ANGLO PERSIAN
LIQUID FUEL
AGENTS, SHAWWALL

694 Oil tanks at Madras set alight by shelling from the guns of SMS *Emden*.

681 SMS *Emden* 'lit' so as to show clearly the radio aerial rigging.

690 The communications station at Direction Island. The radio mast can be clearly seen.

688 HMAS *Sydney.*

701 Captain John C.T. Glossop, captain
HMAS *Sydney.*

698 Barrel of one of the quick-firing 6-inch guns of
HMAS *Sydney.* The paint has peeled from the
gun barrel because of heating up during the
two and a half hour shelling of the *Emden.* The
photograph was taken shortly after the fight.

702 A boat leaves the *Sydney* for the beached
Emden with surrender terms in a letter:

Sir,
I have the honour to request that in the name of humanity you
now surrender your ship to me. In order to show how much I
appreciate your gallantry, I will recapitulate the position.
(1) You are ashore, 3 funnels and 1 mast down and most guns
disabled.
(2) You cannot leave this island and my ship is intact.
In the event of your surrendering, in which I venture to
remind you is no disgrace but rather your misfortune, I will
endeavour to do all I can for your sick and wounded and take
them to a hospital.

I have the honour to be, Sir,
Your obedient servant,
Captain John Glossop.

700 *Emden* in shallow waters, run aground to avoid her sinking, after being severely
damaged by HMAS *Sydney* at the Battle of Cocos, 9 November 1914.

695 A Royal Navy boat from the *Sydney* is rowed out to the grounded *Emden*.
697 Returning ships boat containing prisoners from the *Emden*.

693 A wounded German sailor on the deck of the *Emden*.

723 The landing party from the *Emden*. Under their commander, *Leutnant zur See* Hellmuth von Mücke, they have just destroyed the cable station on the Cocos islands when HMAS *Sydney* arrives and *Korvettenkapitän* Karl Friedrich Max von Müller has to do battle.

725 Men of the landing party watch developments out at sea. Their ship, the *Emden*, has had to leave them and turn to engage the *Sydney*. Relations between the German raiding party and the islanders was cordial. Here we see one of the cable staff sat on the roof of the wireless station with some German officers watching the fighting out at sea.

726 The landing party have a grandstand view of the fighting out at sea. The *Emden* was severely damaged and her captain ran her aground to stop her sinking.

24 The wireless office on Cocos Keeling Island after the visit of the German landing party from the *Emden*. Rolls of message paper are scattered about the floor.

699 The landing party from the *Emden* under their commander, von Mücke, making good their escape in the commandeered old three-masted schooner, *Ayesha*, seen here on the right.

703 Prisoners from the *Emden* exercising on the deck of a British warship. Also on deck (seen beneath the gun barrel in civilian hat) is Captain von Müller. The other man in that group, also wearing civilian clothing with a telescope under his arm, is Prince Francis Joseph of Hohenzollern, a member of the Kaiser's family and serving as a lieutenant on the German commerce raider.

727 On 17 November 1914 HMAS *Sydney* arrived in Colombo Harbour. The five-funnelled cruiser on the right is the Russian cruiser *Askold* and the three-funnelled ship beyond the *Askold* is a converted Pacific liner.

683 On the riddled deck of the *Emden* looking towards the prow.
689 *Emden* looking along the port side towards the prow.

680 Standing off from the wrecked German raider is HMAT *Miltiades*, a British merchant ship leased to the Commonwealth for use as an Australian troop transport at the beginning of the war.

687 *Emden* rear fire control position with wrecked guns.

684 *Emden* looking aft.

686 Smashed state of the wheelhouse and bridge of the *Emden*.

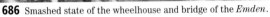

706 Hole in the deck of HMAS *Sydney* made by a shell. It exploded in the Boys' Mess Deck.

685 Bridge of the *Emden* looking aft and showing two of her 4-inch guns port and starboard.

708 How wounded were transferred from ship to land or ship to ship. This transfer of wounded took place after the sinking of HMS *Pegasus* by the German cruiser SMS *Königsberg* at Zanzibar harbour, 20 September.

709 British sailors gathered round for the auction of the effects of a shipmate who has died at sea. Proceeds to be sent to the next of kin.

704 Damaged after-control-platform of HMAS *Sydney*.

705 HMAS *Sydney* had her upper bridge, complete with range finder, shot away.

710 On the morning of 26 November HMS *Bulwark* was lying at anchor in Kethole Reach, Sheerness when an enormous explosion occurred near the after gun turret. Seconds later an even larger explosion ripped the ship apart as its magazines blew up; when the huge pall of smoke cleared there was nothing to be seen. Out of 750 men on board at the time there were just twelve survivors. After investigation enemy action was ruled out and it was noted that at the time a party was working in the after magazines stowing cordite charges. Eventually, because of similar incidents, concerns over British cordite grew and especially was this the case after the Battle of Jutland in 1916.

716 The *Liberty* owned by Courtenay Charles Evan Morgan, 1st Viscount Tredegar, was requisitioned by the Royal Navy for use as a hospital ship.

711, 712, 713 Hospital ship *Rohilla* bound for Dunkirk from Leith floundered on rocks off Whitby in a fierce gale. Lifeboats from Shields and Whitby saved 146 out of 220 persons.

715 German cruiser SMS *Yorck* ran into a minefield guarding after returning from the attack on Yarmouth on 3/4 November. The captain made a navigational error in heavy fog and accidentally sailed into a German defensive minefield. The ship sank quickly with heavy loss of life. Captain Piper, was among those rescued. In December 1914, he was subjected to a court-martial and convicted of negligence.

The Battle of the Falkland Islands took place 8 December 1914. After the Royal Navy defeat at the Battle of Coronel the previous month, a large task force was despatched by the Admiralty to seek out and destroy the victorious Imperial German cruiser squadron.

Commanding the German squadron of two armoured cruisers, SMS *Scharnhorst* and *Gneisenau*, the three light cruisers SMS *Nürnberg*, *Dresden* and *Leipzig*, and three auxiliaries, was Admiral Graf Maximilian von Spee. The German commander decided to raid the British supply base at Stanley and thereby placed his force in danger. A larger British squadron consisting of the battlecruisers HMS *Invincible* and *Inflexible*, the armoured cruisers HMS *Carnarvon*, *Cornwall* and *Kent*, and the light cruisers HMS *Bristol* and *Glasgow* had arrived at the port of Stanley only the day before. Visibility was at its maximum. The advance cruisers of the German squadron were detected at first light and by 9 o'clock that morning the British battlecruisers and cruisers were sailing out to meet the five German ships.

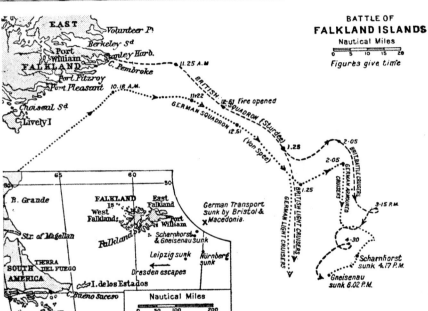

BATTLE OF FALKLAND ISLANDS
Nautical Miles
Figures give time

720 SMS *Scharnhorst* German flag-ship was sunk by HMS *Invincible* and HMS *Inflexible*.

The Yarmouth Raid took place on 3 November 1914, when elements of the German Navy shelled the town of Great Yarmouth. Little damage was done to the town as most shells exploded on the beach. The raid was carried out by the German battlecruiser squadron commanded by Admiral Franz von Hipper with the battlecruisers SMS *Seydlitz*, *Von der Tann* and *Moltke* and *Blücher* and the light cruisers SMS *Strassburg*, *Graudenz*, *Kolberg* and *Stralsund*.

717 HMS *Halcyon* one of the defenders of Great Yarmouth.

718 HMS *Niger* was torpedoed 11 November at Deal by *U12*. One man was killed in the explosion.

719 Captain of the *Niger* Lt-Commander A.P. Muir (inset).

721 Admiral Graf Maximilian von Spee went down with his ship. There were no survivors, including Spee's two sons.

728 Sunk in the Battle of the Falkland Islands, the German cruiser SMS *Nürnberg*.

730 Three ships of the British Squadron, HMS *Kent*, *Inflexible*, and *Glasgow* viewed from the bridge of HMS *Invincible* as they sail out of Port Stanley en route to engage the German squadron.

722 Vice-Admiral Sir Frederick Charles Doveton Sturdee, victor at the Falkland Islands.

1914

315

732 Boats from HMS *Inflexible* picking up survivors from SMS *Gneisenau* after the Battle of the Falkland Islands.

729 Light cruiser SMS *Leipzig* sunk in the Battle of the Falkland Islands.

731 SMS *Leipzig* escaped destruction at the Falkland Islands but was caught at Juan Fernandez and surrendered. She is seen here flying white flags. Before the British could board her she was scuttled by her crew.

733 British sailors feeding a gun aboard one of His Majesty's battle-ships.

734 A Royal Navy Dreadnaught Class battleship on the turn and cleared for action.

735 HMS *Queen Mary* firing her 13.5 inch guns.

736 A torpedo being launched from a destroyer's deck tube.

737 A lone East
Coast sentry.

Following the declaration of war in 1914 every vessel in the waters off the East Coast of England was suspected of being the enemy about to invade. False alarms were sounded regularly. Even Boy Scouts were lent to the Coast-Guard service and were employed in patroling stretches of coastline. In preparation to repel the Kaiser's invading Armies, trenches were dug on the cliff tops and manned by elements of the Territorial Army.

742 Boy Scouts gave a valuable service as observers watching the sea.

738 Guarding England's shores men of a Territorial battalion take a stint in the trenches.

739 Looking out for the German invasion, a group of fishermen and soldiers watching some harmless boat off the East Coast.

740 One of many mounted patrols on the East Coast in the winter of 1914.

741 Ceaseless vigil was maintained by British sailors. A cutter is seen here pulling towards a merchantman to examine its papers.

743 Target coastline published in a German magazine.

746 German sailors fixing shell detonators.

747 East Coast port of Hartlepool was bombarded for thirty-five minutes by cruisers *Seydlitz*, *Blücher* and *Moltke*.

744 Imperial Navy squadron steaming towards the East Coast towns of England.

749 Rear Admiral Franz Ritter von Hipper got permission to raid.

745 Vice Admiral Ingenohl, agreed to the raid.

748 SMS *Moltke* at full steam ahead. *Seydlitz*, *Blücher* and *Moltke* attacked Hartlepool. *Derfflinger, Von der Tann* and *Kolberg* shelled Scarborough.

750 SMS *Kolberg* laid 100 mines off Flambrough Head during the raid. Mines being taken through the Kiel Canal for laying in the North Sea.

752 SMS *Kolberg*.

755 German squadron sailing for the East Coast of England.

756 SMS *Von der Tann.* She was designed in response to the British *Invincible* class.

751 SMS *Seydlitz.*

753 Artist's impression of Scarborough during the bombardment for *The War Illustrated*, issue dated 26 December 1914.

762 Scarborough's medieval defences, the castle walls, breached by 20th Century cannon.

768 The barracks in Scarborough castle yard destroyed.

764 A boarding house on St Nicholas Cliff.

765 A house in Lonsdale Dale.

766 A house on the Esplanade where a shell passed through it and two other dwellings before becoming embeded in a garden without exploding.

761 Scarborough castle keep hit by shells which failed to explode.

757 Scarborough lighthouse takes a direct hit.

767 The Grand Picture Palace, fronting the sea on the cliffs, took a shell which failed to explode.

763 A corner of the Royal Hotel showing damage caused by a shell which failed to explode.

769 Inside one of the houses hit by a shell.

772 Where a family perished. The house in Wykeham Street where a Mrs Barnett and her two children were killed.

772 The Grand Hotel was struck by three shells which failed to explode. This is the restaurant and buffet.

773 A house in Commercial Street.

774 John Shields Ryalls, youngest victim of the raid – 15 months old.

771 Offices at Kingscliffe Camp overlooking South Bay.

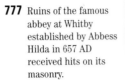

758 Whitby Signal Station wrecked by a direct hit.

777 Ruins of the famous abbey at Whitby established by Abbess Hilda in 657 AD received hits on its masonry.

776 Whitby abbey of St Hilda was targetted.

779 Artist's impression of the attack on Hartlepool.

781 Damage to the rear of a house at Hunter Street Hartlepool.

775 A shell landed on the doorstep of this house in Whitby and tore into the cellars of these two houses.

778 Artist's impression by Matania depicting the incident at the Baptist chapel, West Hartlepool.

778 Baptist chapel, West Hartlepool.

780 Cleveland Road Hartlepool.

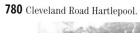

782 Ruins of one of the two gasometers destroyed at Hartlepool.

783 Exterior of a house in Rugby Terrace, West Hartlepool.

784 Interior of a house in Rugby Terrace, West Hartlepool.

785 Lieutenant Colonel Robson commanded the Durham Royal Artillery manning the forts at Hartlepool.

760 Men of the Durham Royal Artillery at practice with a dummy gun. Defences were very weak: two 6-inch guns in the Heugh Battery; a single 6-inch gun at the Lighthouse position and two 4.7-inch guns at South Gare situated across the Tees estuary.

789 Mary Street, Hartlepool.

791 Business premises, Hartlepool.

786 One of many postcards produced at the time. Note the composition of this example: children are posed in front of the damaged church wall. The message is unmistakeable, 'this is what the German Navy gunners were aiming at, children and churches'.

Bombardment of Hartlepools, Dec. 16th, 1914.
St. Barnabas, Hart Road.

BOMBARDMENT OF THE HARTLEPOOLS
DEC. 16TH. 1914. MAINSFORTH TERRACE.

787 Shock of England under bombardment could barely be taken in by the people in this country. Another postcard publicizing the perceived atrocity.

788 Sapper Campbell, Royal Engineers, wounded by a shell fragment – a legitimate target?

792 First man of Kitchener's Army to be killed, Private Theo Jones, died manning Hartlepool defences.

INNOCENT VICTIMS OF GERMAN "KULTUR."

Hartlepool victims of German raid. (1) Geo. Ed. Dixon (killed); (2) Harold Cook and Wilfred Cook (killed); (3) Albt. Dixon (killed); (4) Thos. Heslop (killed); (5) Miss Cause (killed); (6) Margaret Dixon (killed); (7) Mrs. Hannah Arnold (killed) and her daughter Elizabeth (wounded); (8) John M. Whitecross (wounded); (9) Mrs. Edith Jackson (killed) and her daughter Florence (wounded).

REMEMBER SCARBOROUGH!

ENLIST NOW

794 The German raid on the East Coast served as a boost to recruiting. The attack resulted in 137 deaths and 592 injuries, most were civilians.

790 A page from *The War Budget* magazine, 2 January 1915 issue depicting some of the women and children killed and wounded in the raid on Hartlepool.

795 Some of the German shells which failed to explode in the raid on Hartlepool.

796 A Royal Navy Air Service Short Type 74 being catapulted from the launch platform of a British warship.

798 An artist's impression of the British raid.

797 Hoisting a seaplane aboard a British cruiser.

The Cuxhaven Raid was a British ship-based air-raid on the German naval forces at Cuxhaven mounted on Christmas Day, 1914. Aircraft were carried to within striking distance by seaplane tenders of the Royal Navy, supported by both surface ships and submarines. The aircraft flew over Cuxhaven and dropped their bombs causing damage to shore installations.

For the first time in history a naval attack was delivered simultaneously above, on, and from below the surface of the water.
Damage to Cuxhaven was insignificant and the only positive aspect of the raid was the absence of losses for British naval units involved.

799 Contemporary map showing the German naval base with Cuxhaven at the top right.

800 A Royal Navy vessel specially modified to take on board aircraft.

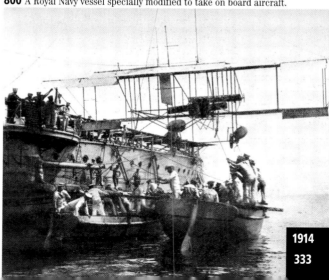

803 A seaplane being conveyed to her parent ship.

804 A seaplane carrier.

801 Flight Commander Theodore Francis Hewlett. After a flight of over three hours, he was compelled to descend on account of engine trouble, but was rescued by a Dutch trawler and landed in Holland, from where he returned safely to England.

802 An Admiralty type 135 two-seater.

805 A painting by Norman Wilkinson of the Cuxhaven raid. It was copied from an English journal and printed in the magazine *Der Krieg 1914/16 in Wort und Bild* with the caption: An English version of their cruisers steaming to Cuxhaven.

Chapter Nine: Trench Warfare – Christmas and Not Over Yet

806 Royal Fusiliers in support trenches near Ploegsteert in Belgium.

807 Germans manning a simply-constructed front line trench at the outset of trench warfare on the Western Front.

808 French army cooks in their dugout, December 1914.

809 British Tommies enjoying their food outside their dugout in the winter of 1914.

815 British cavalry cleaning their equipment during the first fall of snow.

816 Officers wearing recently issued capes and rubber boots.

810 British soldiers bailing out the trench.

812 Trenches at La Boutillerie occupied by men from the Royal Scots Fusiliers.

811 British soldiers keeping their heads down during a bailing out of the trench.

842 The war against water which streamed down the trench sides and flooded over the duckboards.

843 A British soldier takes his turn at the hand-pump in the daily battle against being flooded out.

817 A sentry on outpost duty in the British trenches.

820 Attempting to draw German sniper fire.

818 German sniper watched by a comrade.

819 German sniper at work overseen by an officer.

821 German observation post on top of a haystack.

824 Bringing up a heavy mortar.

822 Pumping out water from the bottom of a trench.

825 German infantry entering a billet after a stint in the trenches.

826 Out of the line an impromptu band performs

823 German infantry in the front line grabbing a brief sleep.

821 German observation equipment in operation behind the lines. The hyposcope was, in effect, a large periscope. An attractive and easy target for enemy artillery.

827 German troops marching off to occupy the trenches. They have been equipped with waders to help them cope with the water-logged conditions.

829 In some sectors trench system construction began to be more substantial. In this French rear area trench the width is sufficient to allow two barrows to pass.

831 In a search for comfort French troops have built dugouts high in the trench and packed them with straw.

834 Marching to take their turn in the trench system stretching across France.

836 Trench periscopes were employed by combatants on both sides.

830 Rolls of chicken wire are being used by these French soldiers to help stabilize dugout walls and for shoring up sides of trenches.

837 A French soldier stands guard at the side of the road while his comrades rest. The original caption suggests that the men have fallen out during their unit's route march to the front lines. The rifles are the Lebel 1886 M93.

840 French take up firing positions in a wrecked graveyard.

835/838 The Royal Artillery bringing up a battery of 4.7" guns in the pouring rain.

844 British Royal Artillery gun crew awaiting orders for another bombardment with their 60-pounder.

849 British 18-pounder gun crew in action. Man on the left is setting the fuse timer.

841 A British motorcycle unit takes up an ambush position at a bend in the road.

839 Men of a British patrol halt to pay their respects before the graves of two men of the 1st Loyal North Lancashire Regiment.

853 Trying to persuade a mule to cooperate.

846 Royal Army Medical Corps unit on the road.

854 Powerful draught horses of the Army Service Corps being exercised.

856 British cavalrymen cleaning and repairing harnesses.

857 Former R.S.P.C.A. inspectors working with the Army Veterinary Corps at the Front.

845 A British army mobile water purifier for drinking and cooking purposes.

859 A British veterinary surgeon attends to a wound.

858 A cavalry sergeant is having his mount re-shod.

855 Indian Army mule baggage column carrying supplies to the front.

860 A Tommy amuses his mates with a story while two others keep an eye on the enemy.

852 British officers at their meal in a dugout which serves as a battalion headquarters for the Cameronians .

813 British soldiers operating a Maxim machine gun from behind a hedge in Flanders. This photograph was released to the press and carried the caption on the back: 'Winter scene in France' and is dated 7 December 1914. Snow had come early in that year.

861 Lunch time in the trenches.

863 Men of the Scots Greys in tented billets.

862 Lunch time in the trenches.

851 British troops wearing the latest goatskin fashion for the trenches.

867 Officers of the Cameronians outside their dugout (see pic 852).

868 Germans in white fur coats issued for sentry duty.

869 British officers have 'bagged' something extra for the pot. Note the double barrelled shot gun.

871 A French liaison officer looks on as 'Tommies' prepare a welcome addition to their officers' rations.

873 Operating a listening device.

865 December near Ploegsteert Wood in Belgium, these British soldiers of the Royal Dublin Fusiliers try to keep warm. Note the rum jar: rum was thought to warm the body.

870 Writing home: a British officer, in a billet out of the line, in a hay loft above a cow shed.

866 Official winter issue.

872 A British soldier in his 'funk' hole. Note that his rifle is cocked (safety catch is on) ready for sudden action.

874 A British staff sergeant and a lieutenant watching the German trenches through the stalks of unharvested sugar beet.

877 Underground dwellings behind the British front line trenches.

875 A view through the sugar beet, British barbed wire towards the German front line.

876 Behind the British front line trenches men attempted to keep warm in December 1914 in the lead up to Christmas. Smoke could attract German shells.

882 Belgians find a dry spot in a water-logged trench and open a Christmas parcel.

848 A French soldier attempts a traditional English dish – Christmas pudding.

878 British soldiers at football.

881 Long hours of boredom in bitter winter conditions were experienced by men on both sides. British soldiers enjoy a welcome distraction and pose for a group photograph in their winter gear.

880 British sergeants pose for the camera with war trophies – German Picklehaub helmet – a much sought after souvenir.

847 Men of a cavalry unit collect mistletoe to decorate their huts.

885 Christmas gifts for the local French children.

893 Base for mail arriving in France.

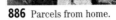

886 Parcels from home.

PRINCESS MARY'S CHRISTMAS GIFT TO THE SOLDIERS AND SAILORS : THE LID OF THE BRASS TOBACCO-BOX.

There is a tasteful and appropriate design on the lid of the brass boxes which will contain Princess Mary's Christmas present of tobacco to the bluejackets and troops. In the centre is a profile relief of the Princess, with the words "Imperium Britannicum," above, and "Christmas 1914" below. At the sides and corners are the names of our Allies—France, Russia, Belgium, Japan, Serbia, and Montenegro. Princess Mary's Fund recently reached £131,000.

900 British troops with their Christmas cards around a decorated tree.

850 Lid of the tobacco tin along with the original caption for the Christmas gift.

894 Princess Mary organized a Christmas box for all army and navy personnel serving.

896 Germans drink a Christmas toast together.

1914
358

892 Sorting Christmas cards to be despatched to the battalions.

899 Collecting parcels for his mates.

897 The sign announces it to be licensed premises. The owner of the estaminet pours a Christmas drink.

895 German officers in a dugout with their decorated tree.

901 Germans decorating their Christmas tree.

887 Germans on Christmas Eve. Next day these same men would instigate a truce.

902 British climb out of their trenches.

888 Some German soldiers had worked in London before the war and chatted with ease.

905 A snap shot of some who took part.

903 One location where the truce took place.

904 Enemies begin to mingle on Christmas Day 1914.

906 An exchange of gifts took place and photographs were taken.

891 Football matches were played.

879 Behind the German lines this choir sings Christmas Carols.

Friday, January 8, 1915.

The Daily Mirror

CERTIFIED CIRCULATION LARGER THAN ANY OTHER DAILY NEWSPAPER IN THE WORLD

WHY DELAY? THE DAILY MIRROR OVERSEAS WEEKLY EDITION contains all the Latest and Best War Pictures and News, and is therefore the Best Weekly Newspaper for your friends abroad. You can obtain it from your Newsagent for 3d. per copy. Subscription rates (prepaid), post free, to Canada for six months 10 , elsewhere abroad 15 . Address—Manager, "Overseas Daily Mirror," 23-29, Bouverie Street, London, E.C.

AN HISTORIC GROUP: BRITISH AND GERMAN SOLDIERS PHOTOGRAPHED TOGETHER.

Foes became friends on Christmas Day, when the British and Germans arranged an unofficial truce. The men left the trenches to exchange cigars and cigarettes, and were even photographed together. This is the historic picture, and shows the soldiers of the opposing Armies standing side by side.

884 In the weeks following Christmas news of the unofficial truce appeared in the press. The British public were left to wonder what to make of it.

The Christmas Spirit 1914.
—*New York World.*

883 How the neutral press viewed the Season of Goodwill in 1914. This cartoon, 'The Christmas Spirit' appeared in the *New York World*, 16 January, 1915.

Index

1st Battalion Cameron Highlanders 165
11th Hussars 61, 186, 246
12th Manitoba Dragoons 64
2nd Dragoons 215

A

aircraft 240–1, 333
Albatross, HMS 25
Albrecht, General 199
Aldershot 23, 58, 61, 156
Alexandra (Royal yacht) 30–1
Alfonso XIII of Spain 9
Allenby, Major General Sir 156
ammunition 100, 106, 168, 204
Amphion, HMS 274–5
Antwerp 79, 93, 100, 110–14, 116, 118–21,
    124–7, 129–35, 142–3
Ariadne, SMS 284
arms 7, 22, 39, 79, 86, 134, 199, 209, 308
army exercises 20–1
artillery 7, 20–3, 36, 41–2, 49, 97, 104, 122, 127,
    136, 163, 169–71, 177, 180, 182, 193–4, 209,
    214, 219–20, 225–8, 244, 250–1, 257, 271, 330,
    341, 345–6
Asquith, Herbert 40
assassins 28, 32, 36
attack 91–2, 111, 144, 172, 174, 202, 282, 284–5,
    288, 300, 314, 328, 332
Audacious, HMS 298
Austria 7, 26, 32, 39
Austro-Hungarian Empire 6–7, 37–40, 42

B

battalions 46–7, 54, 79, 103, 168, 261, 263, 359
battle 74, 79, 81, 83, 86, 88, 98, 114, 182, 195,
    200, 212, 221, 227, 288, 300, 306, 314–16
battlecruisers 288, 314–15
battleships 9, 14, 17, 22, 282
bayonet 7, 22, 61, 239, 258
Belgian Government 119, 121
Belgian Lancers 100
Belgians 40, 94, 99–100, 113–15, 124, 126, 128,
    151, 153–4, 271, 356
Belgium 7, 9, 40, 68, 88, 91–2, 102, 107, 123,
    138, 146, 158–9, 162–3, 170, 246, 257, 270, 335
Belgrade 38–9

Bengal Lancers 64, 215
Berlin 41, 44–5, 52, 64, 72, 88
billets 253, 256, 267, 340, 353
Birmingham, HMS 276–7
Black Watch 156, 266
Blücher, SMS 315, 320–1
boats 25, 116–17, 129, 212, 304, 316
Boer War 60
bombardment 108, 249–50, 323, 331, 346
Boulogne 103–5, 156, 187–8
Boy Scouts 47, 72, 200, 319
Britain 6–7, 11–12, 25, 40, 51, 54, 114, 288
British Army 12–13, 22, 62, 79–80, 105, 164
British Expeditionary Force (BEF) 64–5, 102,
    132, 156, 212, 269
British soldiers 70, 88, 103, 110, 158, 166,
    172–3, 223, 249–50, 252, 256–7, 336–7, 351–3,
    356, 358
Brussels 93, 95, 97–8, 121–3, 127

C

Cabrinoviç, Nedeljko 35–6
Calais 116
Cameronians 177–9, 212, 217, 225, 350, 352
Canada 63, 66
cavalry 7, 91, 103, 162, 164, 194
chaplains 86, 88
Charleroi 99
children 7, 32, 41, 87, 118, 326, 331–2
China 10
Christchurch 66–7
Christmas 5, 53, 333, 335, 355–9, 361–2
Churchill, Winston 6, 12, 14–15
Claustrum St Martini 249, 251
Coldstream Guards 266
comrades 78, 89, 120, 339
conspirators 32, 34, 36
Constanza 26–7
Cressy, HMS 297
crew 86, 194, 274, 276–7, 293, 300, 302, 316, 346
cruisers 284, 287–8, 296, 299–300, 302, 314
Cubriloviç, Vaso 36
Cubriloviç, Veljko 36–7

D

d'Espéray, General 198
damage 125, 285, 302, 315, 326, 328, 333

dead 34, 197, 208, 210–11, 223, 230, 245, 258, 302

death 11, 36–7, 332

Deguise, Lt Gen 118

Derfflinger, SMS 321

Despatch riders 160, 181, 192

destroyers 30–1, 275, 288

Devonshire House 69

Dorrell, Sgt Maj 181–2

Doullens 185–6

Dover 130, 299

dreadnaught 14, 16, 22, 31

Dreadnaught, HMS 14–15

E

dugout 231, 336, 342, 350, 352, 359

Egypt 66–7

Emden, SMS 302–3

enemy 91, 115, 158, 178, 205–6, 222, 246, 259, 264, 267, 319, 350, 361

England 4, 13–14, 47, 57, 86, 116–17, 134, 214, 321, 331, 334

Europe 6, 9, 46–7, 64, 67

explosion 312, 315

F

Falkland Islands 300, 314–16

Fearless, HMS 284

Ferdinand, King 9, 26–7, 32–4, 36–7

field gun 23, 81, 128, 171, 180, 196–7, 215, 225, 228, 238

fighting 4–5, 9, 11, 31, 38, 65, 68, 88, 102, 108–9, 119, 154, 172, 181, 191, 209–10, 220–3, 225, 227, 259, 266–7, 273, 280, 285, 301–2, 304, 306

firing positions 97, 109, 171, 197, 215, 247, 276, 300, 302, 345

First World War 36

fleet 30–1, 71, 94, 105, 129, 288

Foch, General 13, 198

food 123, 138, 143, 336

Foster, Lt Frank 57

Fox, Lt Col 84

France 7, 22, 40, 68, 80, 88, 90, 102, 114, 156, 158, 160, 182, 199, 204, 212, 214, 221, 240, 262–3, 268, 342, 358

Frederick VII of Denmark 9

French, Field Marshal Sir John 198

front line 39, 225, 335, 341, 354–5

G

Galliéni, General Joseph 200–1

gasometers 329

German Army 19–20, 76, 78, 91–2, 96, 99, 118, 127, 141, 150, 155, 158, 173–4, 180–1, 196, 206, 221, 224, 258–9, 270, 340–1

German invaders 192–3

German Navy 130, 142, 280, 282–3, 290, 315, 320, 331

German officers 123, 127, 143, 152, 228, 231, 306, 359

German prisoners 157, 213, 218, 268, 275

German troops 7, 72, 87, 107, 113, 121–2, 170, 208, 229–30, 341, 360

Germans 74, 83, 101, 108, 110, 113–14, 116, 119, 123, 126, 132, 134, 144, 146, 148, 162, 172, 176–7, 183, 186, 192, 197, 208, 210, 212, 214, 220, 223, 230, 233, 236–7, 256–7, 259, 264–5, 270–2, 276, 282, 352, 359

Germany 6–7, 9, 12–13, 40, 51, 63, 75, 125

Gheluvelt 247, 264–5

Ghent 101, 136, 140, 247

Glasgow 29, 64, 314–15

Glasgow, HMS 300

Gneisenau, SMS 301, 316

Good Hope, HMS 300

Gough, Lt Gen 258

Grenadier Guards 102

guns 14–15, 22, 31, 36, 42, 49, 100, 109, 124, 127, 144, 148–9, 171, 181, 183, 195, 204, 214, 225, 267, 269, 276, 278, 295, 301–4, 309–10, 317, 330, 345

H

Haakon VII of Norway 9

Haig, General Sir Douglas 156

Halcyon, HMS 315

Hartlepool 320, 328–30, 332

Hawke, HMS 298

Heeringen, General 199

Hela, SMS 295

Heligoland Bight 280, 282, 284, 286–8, 290, 295

Hellmuth von Mücke, Lt sur See 302, 306

Hermes, HMS 299

Highflyer, HMS 279
Hogue, HMS 297
Holland 116, 129, 134, 334
horses 95, 97, 106, 116, 156–7, 180, 182, 193, 209, 226, 236, 250
hospital 33–4, 190, 304
hospital ship 70, 187, 312
Hyde Park 14, 54–5

I

Iliç, Danilo 36–7
Indian Ocean 294, 302–3
Inflexible, HMS 314, 316
invaders 18, 93, 98, 104, 111, 121, 128, 184, 204, 212, 220
Iron Duke, HMS 31
Italy 6–7, 28, 38

J

Jellicoe, Admiral 284, 288
Joffre, General 198
Jovanoviç, Misko 36

K

Kaiser, The 6–7, 10, 12–13, 16, 22, 38, 45, 72–3, 102, 108, 199, 279–82, 288, 290, 308, 319
Kaiserin, SMS 290
Keyes, Commodore Roger 288–9
King Albert 114, 128
King George 12–13, 28–9, 31, 51, 61
King's Liverpool Regiment 61
Kitchener, Lord 53–4, 56, 60–1
Kolberg, SMS 315, 321–2
Köln, SMS 288
Königin Luise, SMS 274–5
Königsberg, SMS 294–5, 310

L

La Boutillerie 337
La Ferté-sous-Jouarre 212
Lagny 212–13
Lake Constance 15, 124–5
Langle de Cary, General 198
Le Havre 119, 121, 188
Lee-Enfield 22
Lee-Metford 60
Leicestershire Regiment 60, 159

Leipzig, SMS 316
Liberty, HMS 284
Lincoln, Abraham 28
Lincolnshire Regiment 58
Lion, HMS 286–8
Lisbon 28
London 8, 41, 47, 51, 53, 55, 69–70, 80, 190, 360
London Regiment 55, 160, 261–2
London Scottish 261–7
London Territorials 77, 79
Lord Derby of Liverpool 60

M

machine guns 98, 100, 106, 127, 144, 148, 169, 174, 204, 241, 267, 269
Mainz, SMS 284–5, 288
march 92, 158, 193, 200, 220, 239, 265
Marie Leonhardt, SMS 63
Marines 38, 116, 120
Marlborough, HMS 31
Marne, river 5, 114, 186, 191, 195, 200–1, 208–9, 212–13
Maunoury, General 198
men 46, 49, 55–6, 67, 102, 135, 159, 177, 182, 186, 209, 235, 253, 259–60, 262, 306, 330, 347, 351, 357
Messines 264–7
Middlesex Regiment 55, 61, 80
Miljacka, river 35
mines 291, 322
Moltke, SMS 315, 320–1
Monmouth, HMS 300–1
Mons 5, 155–6, 158–9, 161–8, 172–3, 175–7, 181–2, 190
Mons-Condé canal 164, 167
Munich 52
murder 32, 36, 39

N

Nassau, SMS 16
nations 4, 6–7, 10–11, 14, 26, 38, 53
new recruits 23, 54, 58, 60, 261
New Zealand, HMS 31, 286
Nieuport 154, 272
Niger, HMS 315
North Sea 9, 270, 273–4, 277, 288–9, 322

Northumberland Hussars 254
Nürnberg, SMS 300–1, 314–15

O
officers 39, 61, 75, 154, 266, 275–6, 302, 336, 339, 352
Ostend 106, 115–16, 131, 136

P
Pankurst, Emmeline 29
parcels 358–9
Paris 63, 73, 86, 139, 177, 186, 191–2, 198, 200–2, 208–9, 212, 218
Pathfinder, HMS 292–3
Pegasus, HMS 295, 310
Peking 7
Picklehaube helmets 213, 357
Ploegsteert Wood 353
Plymouth 70
Pope Benedict XV 76
Pope Pius X 76
Portsmouth 48–9, 70–1
positions 31, 34, 104, 110, 119, 169, 173, 197, 205, 222, 232, 271, 304
priests 79, 86, 97
Prince of Wales 51
Princip, Gavrilo 32, 34–7
prisoners 10–11, 183, 218, 288, 302, 305, 308

Q
Queen Mary, HMS 286, 317

R
raid 288, 314–15, 321–2, 327, 332–3
rations 108, 140, 352
Rawlinson, General 60
recruiting offices 7, 51, 54, 62
Red Army 18–19
Red Cross 69, 92, 97
refugees 97, 101, 116
Robertson, Lt Col 178
Romania 26–7
Royal Dublin Fusiliers 353
Royal Engineers 18, 48, 172, 212, 235, 331
Royal Flying Corps 149, 156, 240
Royal Fusiliers 55, 167, 182, 335

Royal Horse Artillery 182
Royal Naval Division 110–11, 120, 129, 134–5
Royal Naval Flying Corps 242
Royal Navy 24–5, 279, 284–5, 287–9, 296–7, 305, 312, 314, 333
Royal Scots Fusiliers 247, 337
Russia 6–7, 12, 27, 40, 42, 74, 77, 109
Russians 84, 92

S
sailors 8, 48–9, 70, 134, 281, 288, 292, 296, 298, 302, 305
Sarajevo 32–4
Scarborough castle 324–5
Scharnhorst, SMS 299–300, 314
Scheldt, river 114, 129
Scotland 28, 292–3, 298
Scots Greys 351
Scots Guards 247, 253
scouts 47, 164, 166, 172, 193, 236
Seaforth Highlanders 159
Serbia 28, 36, 38–40, 42
Seydlitz, SMS 315, 320–1, 323
shells 81, 95, 200, 225, 229, 232, 276, 300, 310, 315, 324–7, 329
Smith-Dorrien, General Sir H.L. 18, 157
Soissons 223, 226–7, 229, 232
soldiers 7–8, 10–11, 70, 83, 86, 91, 135, 208, 319
Southampton 102, 262
Spee, Reichsgraf von 299–300, 314–15
Speedy, HMS 292
St Marguerite 225
St Maxence 212
St Vincent, HMS 21
submarines 8, 288, 290, 333
Sukhomlinov, General 42
survivors 267, 275, 288, 292, 300, 312, 315–16
Sydney 302, 304–6, 310
Sydney, HMAS 302, 304, 306, 308, 311

T
Tarter, HMS 25
Tirlemont 97
torpedo 24, 278, 292–5, 298, 317
trenches 5, 22, 56, 152–3, 224, 230, 247, 319, 335, 337, 340–3, 351–2, 354–5, 360

troops 7, 10, 13, 15, 40, 64, 100, 119, 128, 156, 199

tuberculosis 36–7

Tyrwhitt, Commodore Reginald 288

U

Uhlans 138, 184, 236, 257, 264

Usufumo, The 25

victims 8, 298, 327

V

Vienna 36–7, 39, 199

Visé 92, 95, 98, 108

von Beseler, General 111

von Bülow, General 199

von der Tann, SMS 315, 321–2

von Einem, General 199

von Hausen, General 199

von Holtzendorf, Admiral 16

von Kluck, General 199

von Müller, General Alexander 283, 302, 306–7

von Spee, Admiral 314–15

von Tirpitz, Admiral 16

W

war 6–7, 9, 22–3, 26, 30, 40, 42, 45, 47–8, 51–4, 62, 66, 70–1, 74, 79, 84, 86, 134, 143, 149, 152, 231, 274, 276–7, 282, 290, 302, 309, 319, 337, 360

Warwickshire Regiment 264

water 25, 107, 276, 319, 333, 337, 340

West Africa 279

West Hartlepool 329–30

Whitby 313, 328–9

Wilhelmshaven 281–3

women 29, 71–2, 209, 332

Woodcote Camp 57

wounded 35, 68, 70, 79, 96, 139, 141, 187–90, 216, 232, 256, 288, 302, 304–5, 310, 331–2

wounds 95, 99, 181–2, 208, 229, 252, 349

Y

Yorck, SMS 314

Ypres 5, 219, 244, 246–57, 259–60, 264–7, 269

Z

Zeppelin 124–5